Emerald Ark

Memories of a Jewish Irish Youth

Theo Garb

with Michael Garb

Cover Design by Isabella Langer

Copyright © 2023 Michael Garb
All rights reserved.

Dedication

This memoir is lovingly dedicated to my best friend, my wife, Celia, and to the 200 beautiful souls in my family who perished in the Holocaust.

Contents

Introduction	1
Jews in Ireland?	
Chapter 1	7
Wanderings	
Chapter 2	25
Diamonds and Arias	
Chapter 3	35
Manna from Heaven	
Chapter 4	41
Rachel the *Baleboste*	
Chapter 5	43
A Visit with the Shochet	
Chapter 6	49
Matzah Biscuits? Woof!	
Chapter 7	53
My First Day at School	
Chapter 8	57
Seeking Refuge	
Chapter 9	63
The Long Shadows of War	
Chapter 10	71
Hitler's Synagogue	
Chapter 11	79
A Cottage by the Sea	
Chapter 12	89
Father Seamus	
Chapter 13	99
A Boy Becomes a Man	

Chapter 14	109
War's End: Picking Up the Pieces	
Chapter 15	115
Teen Social Groups	
Chapter 16	121
Flirtation Gone Awry	
Chapter 17	127
On a Mission in Belfast	
Chapter 18	135
Romantic Notions	
Chapter 19	141
My Zeyde	
Chapter 20	157
The Disappearance	
Chapter 21	171
Margaret	
Chapter 22	191
A Parting of Ways	
Epilogue	199
Editor's Note	207
Addt'l Photographs	209

Introduction

Jews in Ireland?

Experience has taught me how people will react when I open my mouth to speak, whether at a dinner party, a social function, a lifecycle celebration, in a store – a chance encounter with strangers, anywhere, at any time. No sooner do I speak than a curious look comes over their faces. The accent gets them every time.

"Where are you from?" they'll ask. If I'm feeling playful, I'll have them guess my country of origin: "England? Australia? South Africa?" Sometimes they name places far more exotic. Rarely does anyone guess correctly.

When I answer, "Ireland," I'm often met with disbelief.

"Ireland?"

"Yes, Ireland."

"Dublin?"

"Yes, Dublin."

They'll weigh my answer carefully. When I first came to America in 1950, this was the typical reaction. Sporting jet-black hair and a tanned complexion, my visage contrasted with one's perception of an Irishman. Not so much these days, as my hair has salt-and-peppered, my Irish brogue, softened.

Narrowing their eyes and leaning forward a bit, "You said Dublin."

"Sure, and begorra," I'd smile.

"Then you must be Black Irish," the more astute would say, referring to a people who had come to Ireland centuries ago, known for their dark features.

"No, I'm not Black Irish."

"If you're not Black Irish, then what?"

"I'm an Irish Jew."

"An Irish Jew?"

I might well have said I was the King of Norway – who ever heard of an Irish Jew? In reality, few people have, and I'm somewhat puzzled by this. After all, we Jews have settled in the farthest outposts of the world. China has a Jewish community and, so too, does India. So why not Ireland?

Everyone knows that Ireland is a Catholic country. This truth overshadows my proud heritage. Irish Jews of the past century include such luminaries as:

- Isaac Herzog: Ireland's first Chief Rabbi, 1919–36, Chief Rabbi of Palestine and Israel, 1936–59
- Immanuel Jakobovits: Chief Rabbi of Ireland, 1949–58, Chief Rabbi of Great Britain, 1967–91
- Robert Briscoe: Dublin's first Jewish Lord Mayor, 1956–57, 1961–62
- Chaim Herzog: President of Israel, 1983–93
- Leonard Abrahamson: Gaelic scholar, cardiac surgeon, and professor of medicine, 1920s–1960s
- Mervyn Taylor: a member of Irish Parliament, Minister for Equality and Law Reform, 1993–97

And let's not forget Leopold Bloom, the immortal character from James Joyce's *Ulysses*. Why *not* Ireland?

As Irish Jews, no more than 5,500 of us at any one time, our presence reached far beyond our modest numbers. What tiny community of people has given the world such gifts as have the Jews?

So it was, in Ireland. Hundreds of us enjoyed reputations for excellence in medicine, law, engineering, the arts, and politics. Believe it or not, Irish Jews can boast of their achievements in sports at the international level. For instance, Louis Bookman, Irish footballer and cricketer of the early 20th century; Louis Jacobson, Irish cricketer of the mid-20th century; and Lara Molins, female Irish World Cup cricketer of the 21st century.

Indeed, why *not* Ireland? My Jewish ancestry and Irish homeland are as much a matter of pride for me as they are a fascination for others. When I arrived in America and settled in the Flatbush section of Brooklyn, people would ask if I left Ireland because of antisemitism. The question both surprised and saddened me. At the time, ethnic groups were fighting for a piece of the American dream. The "melting pot" spewed with conflict. This was not the case in Ireland, certainly not Dublin.

Joyce did write of antisemitism in *Ulysses*; however, I encountered none while growing up. In Dublin, I lived in a community of thirty-five hundred Jews. Cork, Limerick, Waterford, and a few other towns had much smaller communities. It may be that Jews were spared a more virulent antisemitism because of the deeper conflicts between Catholics and Protestants, as well as the Irish struggle for independence from England.

How did we Jews come to live in Ireland? The first record, noted in the *Annals of Inisfallen*, dates back to 1079, when a handful of Jewish wanderers made their way over from France. They came bearing gifts for King Tordelbach, but were refused entry and deported home.

After that initial foray, the record is silent until the thirteenth century, when a handful more came over. But it wasn't until the 17th century, when large numbers of Jews arrived from Portugal, that a Jewish community began to take hold in Ireland. In 1660, the first Irish synagogue was built in Dublin.

Throughout the diaspora, Jews have fled one threat or another, searching for peace and stability in their lives. The Spanish Inquisition of 1478–92 forced Spanish and Portuguese Jews to publicly embrace Christianity or be burned at the stake. Some historians believe that Christopher Columbus was a *converso*, a Jew who converted to Catholicism to escape persecution. Those who refused were known as *Marranos* or "hidden" Jews. Some came to Ireland, where they could openly practice their Judaism. In the early 1700s, they were offered land, perhaps three-quarters of an acre, to build a Jewish cemetery. The local township and county Dublin sold them the land for thirty-four pounds, with a thousand-year lease and a rental of one peppercorn per year. This cemetery stands today as a national landmark in Ballybough, north of Dublin.

By the late 19th and early 20th centuries, Jews were fleeing Eastern and Central Europe in great numbers. They sought refuge from discrimination and the violence of *pogroms*. Many came to America, but ships were few, able sailors and precise maps fewer still. Refugees en route to America often landed in Ireland and settled there, charmed by its greenery.

A wave of Jewish immigration occurred after a potato famine ravaged Eire in the mid-19th century. Starvation and disease were rampant and, in addition, British colonial policies caused suffering for Irish families. Many Catholics left Ireland during these years and headed for America. Those who stayed identified with the oppression of the Jews, which encouraged tolerance between the communities.

The Jews and the Irish share a deep affinity, one that dates back to biblical times. While some are familiar with the Druids and shadowy Firbolgs of Irish mythology, they may not know it includes the tale of *Noah's Ark*. The bond between the Irish and the Jews appears most natural in light of shared experience and mystical roots. It is no accident that Ireland is the only country in Europe where Jewish blood has not been spilled as the result of bigotry.

By the early 1900s, Ireland was well-known as a refuge for Jews. It was to this emerald sanctuary that my father, Wolf Garbarz, came with his wife and family in the spring of 1930. In Polish, Garbarz (pron. Garbash) means tanner, that is, someone who tans hides. Along the way, he shortened Garbarz to Garb. It was easier to spell and pronounce and, besides, a man settling in a new land should have a new name to start a new life. Dublin's Orthodox Jewish community, gathered south of the River Liffey, welcomed the Garb clan and embraced Wolf as their cantor. It was here that Cantor Reverend Wolf Garb and his wife, Rachel, would raise their family in peace and openly practice their faith.

Chapter 1
Wanderings

It is true that we Jews wander, but we do not wander aimlessly. Born May 13, 1899, my father, Wolf, grew up in Warsaw, Poland, the eldest of five siblings. The Great War was drawing to a close when, at eighteen, he was drafted into the Polish army and served as secretary to legendary battle commander and statesman, Jozef Pilsudski. The war was not something he spoke of when he recalled those early years of his adulthood. Being a soldier – cannon fodder for a war machine – was not his idea of fulfillment.

Wolf's true gift was evident early on. His sweet child soprano voice would mature into a powerful dramatic tenor. Destined to be a *chazzan,* or cantor, his voice inspired worshippers to tremble with emotion. When he chanted the "Kol Nidre" on Yom Kippur eve, one felt connected to the thousands of years of Jewish experience. On such occasions, the congregation wept openly.

As a boy, Wolf learned the art of *chazzanus* (cantorial singing) from the great cantors of his day and was trained as a young man how best to serve the Jewish community. Poland had long been a center of Jewish learning and worship in Eastern Europe. During his youth, three million Jews lived there, and the capital city of Warsaw thrived with Torah study and prayer. Learned rabbis taught the sacred lessons of our people, and cantors infused prayer services with their golden voices and heartfelt chanting of *tefilah* (prayer).

At nine, to eleven years of age, Wolf performed as a boy-soprano soloist in the choir of The Great Synagogue of Warsaw, commonly known as the Tlomackie *Shul* (synagogue). Aspiring cantors would flock there to listen to and learn from the cantorial masters of Eastern Europe. Cantors of early to mid-20th century renown, like Gershon Sirota, "the Jewish Caruso," Yossele Rosenblatt, and Moshe Koussevitzky, among others, were invited to officiate prayer services there. It was in this august center of Jewish liturgy that my father became Chazzan Sirota's chief choirboy soloist, under the direction of celebrated choirmaster, Leo Lowe.

Though a prodigy, as he approached the age of Bar Mitzvah, the cantor and choirmaster would listen to him sing, with trepidation. There is no more vulnerable time in a male singer's life than the onset of puberty. The voice of an angel could well become the sound of gravel rushing along a dry road. But God had *rachmanos* (mercy) on my father, and his voice became his livelihood. While serving in the military, he would organize open-air concerts in the Citadel, a historic landmark of Warsaw. His repertoire included arias and popular Polish songs of the era. Other soldiers performed as well, accompanied by an army band.

The Great Synagogue of Warsaw (1878–1942)
7 Tlomackie Square, Warsaw, Poland

At the time, my mother's sister, Miriam Rosenstrauch, was dating a man named Pinya, my father's cousin. One day, Miriam took my mother, Rachel, to Pinya's home, where she was introduced to Wolf.

"It was love at first sight," my mother once said during her later years. Rachel Rosenstrauch was a mere twenty years of age, innocent, and open to the enchantment of love. She welcomed my father's courtship and would often meet him on the Citadel grounds.

"Oh, they were lovely, those concerts," she continued, a gentle smile playing on her lips as she recalled those distant summers. "The air was soft against my cheek, and your father, ah! He was so handsome in his uniform, and his voice, beautiful."

Their encounters were dream-like: evening serenades with Wolf in uniform, moonlit walks along the Vistula, Rachel's innocence and charm; they both fell deeply in love and were married in 1921. Wolf was the son of a craftsman, and Rachel, a daughter of wealth and privilege, and yet, the match was encouraged by both their families. In those days, there was great honor in being a servant of God, even if a man was, otherwise, poor.

Wolf Garbarz, Polish Army (1918)

Rachel Rosenstrauch & Wolf Garbarz, Warsaw, Poland (1920)

Wolf's father, Shlomo Tzvi Garbarz, a humble carpenter, raised his five children alone (his wife, Liba, having passed from a bout with tuberculosis in 1919). Rachel's father, Solomon Rosenstrauch, was known as the "Herring King of Warsaw." A successful fish merchant, he bottled and sold a variety of pickled herring throughout Europe. In those days, men came with horse and wagon to collect the bottles and transport them to market. My grandfather was a wholesaler and exporter, but somehow, I like the "Herring King" title best!

Sadly, wherever Jews have settled in the world, there has been antisemitism. While Jews and Poles lived together for a thousand years in mostly peaceful co-existence, in times of economic strife, it was not safe for a Jew to be too prominent or too successful. This alone could invite threats and even physical assaults. Was there an untoward incident that drove this point home to Grandpa Solomon? I cannot say, but he was aware of the dangers. One day, he washed his hands of the fish business and moved his family to Antwerp, Belgium, the diamond capital of the world. There remains proof of his success in the herring enterprise – a two-story apartment building at 45 Targowa, in the Praga district of Warsaw, where my mother and her relatives had lived. To this day, we press our claim to its ownership with the Polish government, as thousands of properties were confiscated by the communist regime after World War II.

"45 Targowa, Warsaw"
The Home of Rachel Rosenstrauch & Family

In the early 1920s, Grandpa Solomon entered the diamond trade in Belgium. Ma would laugh when she spoke of the change. "I don't know which was more lucrative, but I can tell you that I liked the sparkle of diamonds much better than the smell of herring!"

My mother and father lived in Warsaw for a time, in that same building, where their first child, Abraham (Abey), was born on January 12,1924. During my father's stint in the army, the Warsaw government took note of his singing prowess and, after his discharge, placed him on scholarship at the Warsaw Conservatory, where he studied music. As well, he pursued his cantorial training at The Great Synagogue.

Soon after Abey's birth, my parents decided to leave Poland and follow Grandpa Solomon to Belgium. The challenges and, ultimately, the horrors of the European Jewish experience in those years are amply chronicled. Guided by Da's (Dad's) inner compass, they traveled west to escape the impending storm. Married and with child, Ma agreed that it was time for her budding family to leave Poland.

A paradox lay at the heart of Jewish existence wherever one might settle. Orthodox Jews feel obliged to honor tradition: *Kashrut* (keeping kosher), Torah study, and Sabbath and holiday observance. These aspects of faith are impressed upon children by parents who will not deviate from Jewish law. In the same time, observant Jews struggle with tradition in their desire to participate fully in society. Whether in Europe or on other continents of the world, we Jews have always contributed to the dominant culture surrounding us.

This desire to assimilate was tempered by a fear of being hated and discriminated against by society – an essential piece of the magnet that determined my father's compass. His early wanderings were driven by a need for self-preservation; this was a big part of the thrust for joining his in-laws in Antwerp, in 1925.

With his resolve to emigrate, he was not merely fleeing, but heading toward something of worth. For Da, living in Antwerp meant that he could learn the diamond trade, while launching his cantorial career. Such prospects were countered by the distress of leaving his father and siblings behind, who had their own studies and professions to attend to, and who were not about to leave Warsaw.

So it was that my parents settled in Antwerp for three years, where Wolf earned a glowing reputation as a cantor and developed a keen eye for the best diamond offerings. Grandpa Solomon taught my father the industry: how rough stones were cut and shaped, how to judge color and quality, and how to buy and sell. Da worked hard at it; like any responsible family head, he was determined to better his financial status.

Chazzan Rev. Wolf Garbarz, Antwerp, Belgium (1926)

My sister, Lucienne (Lucy), was born in Antwerp on July 9, 1926, another mouth to feed. Da's primary goal was to audition for better paying cantorial positions, wherever they may be found on the European continent. Conversations with Ma ensued; how much longer would they remain in Antwerp? Considering a change, he read an advertisement seeking a cantor for a prominent shul in Holland. Being true to his heart's compass, he answered the ad with dispatch and traveled to Amsterdam, where he moved the congregation with his soulful chanting of sacred prayer.

They offered Wolf the job but made a number of stipulations, one of which, I think, is quite fascinating: my mother would have to wear a *sheitel,* a hairpiece worn by married Jewish women. Ultra-orthodox women, such as in Mea She'arim, Jerusalem, or Borough Park, Brooklyn, still wear such wigs. But for most modern Jewish women, observant or not, the sheitel is an anachronism.

The rationale for the sheitel is derived from the rules of *tz'niut* or modesty. Jewish wives are not to do anything that might attract the lustful attention of men. Because a woman's hair is considered alluring, it is to be hidden, so that only her husband sees it – for only a husband should be attracted to his wife, lest she invites a man to break the commandment against adultery. When Ma heard of this, she was livid.

"Are they suggesting I am not religious enough without a sheitel? I am not cutting my hair!"

Though sympathetic, my father, excited about the position, downplayed my mother's sacrifice. But this was asking too much of her. She was a pretty woman with lovely, long tresses, and her cheeks were now wet with tears.

"Not important? Maybe not to you. You're not the one being asked to chop off your hair."

"There, there," my father said, trying to comfort her. "It will all work out, you'll see."

"Will it?"

In the end, the sheitel requirement prevented my father from accepting the job. They left Antwerp a short time later, en route to a shul and a life in London, England, proving to me that God was watching over our little family. In 1940, Hitler's forces rolled into Holland and decimated the country's Jewish population. If not for my mother's stubborn insistence – some would say vanity – all that follows might never have been.

* * *

After a year in London, my family moved to Manchester in 1928, where a larger congregation awaited us – the Holy Law Synagogue, which is still in existence today, more than one hundred and fifty years after its founding. I was born July 10, 1929, shortly after my father assumed his new post.

Chazzan Rev. Wolf Garbarz, Manchester, England (1929)

Rev. W. Garbarz.
First Reader Holy Law Hebrew Congregation.

                        119, Stocks Street,
                            Cheetham,
                                Manchester.

The Hon. Sec.
   S. Santhouse
     74 Stocks St,
            Cheetham

Dear Sir

I thank you for your letter of the 17th inst. and I have much pleasure in accepting your kind invitation. With Zions Greeting

Yours Sincerely

W. Garbarz

I'm told that my birth went smoothly for my mother, and that I was a lively, alert newborn with my first Jewish rite of passage, my *bris,* just days ahead. The *bris* or *brit milah* is a Jewish tradition dating back to the first Jew, Abraham. According to this covenant, God promised Abraham that his descendants would be ". . . as numerous as the stars in heaven and the sands by the sea." He also promised a homeland for them. Abraham bravely kept his covenant with *Hashem* (God) by removing his own foreskin in a ritual act of circumcision.

This is not the time to explore the depths of Abraham's faith, which allowed him to do such a thing (without anesthesia mind you!). After Abraham, Hashem commanded that this rite be performed on every Jewish male, the eighth day of life. The obligation for this *mitzvah,* or commandment, is upon the father of the boy. Loath to perform this delicate ritual, Jewish fathers contract to have it done by a *mohel* (pron. moyel), a man trained in circumcision.

In addition to being a cantor, Wolf was also a mohel and *shochet,* a butcher qualified to slaughter animals according to kosher dietary laws. I trust that someone prayed the day of my bris that my father would not confuse these skills and be more of a shochet than a mohel! In later years, I came to know that Da was actually a "mohel's mohel." Affectionately known to his peers as "the royal mohel," more than once, he was summoned by the Royal Family, during the reign of King George V, to consult on an ill-performed circumcision.

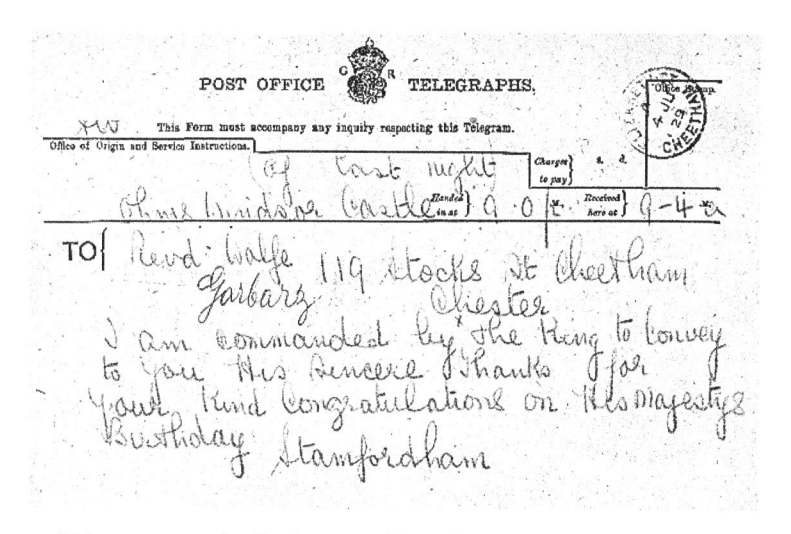

Telegram reads: To Rev. Wolf Garbarz, June 4, 1929, "I am commanded by the king to convey to you His sincere thanks for your kind congratulations on His Majesty's birthday." Stamfordham (Sir Arthur Bigge, Private Secretary to the King)

The heat and dampness of an English July fell upon our home. In the living room, a dignified gathering of men from the community spoke in hushed tones among themselves. The women stood at the periphery – this was tradition. As I was brought into the room, my father shouted, *"Baruch habah!* Blessed is he who enters the covenant." My anesthesia was a piece of cotton gauze dipped in red wine for me to suck on, my cries, a sign that all was well.

Family Garb, Manchester, England (1930)

I came into the world in the city of Manchester, but as fate would have it, we moved to Ireland within the year. My father learned of an opportunity at Dublin's main synagogue, where the cantor had resigned, and the community had begun a search to replace him. More than twenty of Europe's finest cantors sought the position. Da was invited for a trial and won the congregation over. He accepted the job, knowing that Ireland was more than a beautiful country – Hitler's rise to power was gathering steam, and Ireland, which had declared neutrality in World War I, would be a safe haven for our family, if there be another war.

Now with two sons and a daughter, my parents were ever more conscious of the need to protect their family from harm. The Irish had never run to war. The only time they were eager to fight was against the British – this, attributed to the history of Ireland's conquest by England. The Irish revolted in 1916, which led to the creation of an

Irish Free State in 1922. But that flashpoint in history was long past by the time we packed up our house and moved in the spring of 1930. A well-established Dublin Jewish community embraced the Garb clan.

The chief rabbi of Ireland, Yitzchak Halevi Herzog (Isaac Herzog), who was born in Russia, came to Dublin via Belfast. He was a brilliant Torah scholar, said to have learned the *Talmud* (the entire Torah and supplementary texts) by heart in his twenties. Rabbi Herzog and his wife, Sarah, had two sons, Chaim and Yaakov, both born in Ireland, who became distinguished men in their own right. As spiritual leaders of the community, the Herzog and Garb families grew close, and we children played together.

A few years later, on February 8, 1935, my sister, Sarah, was born. We were now four siblings, each hailing from a different country: Abe, born in Poland, Lucy, in Belgium, myself, in England, and Sarah, in Ireland – a truly international family! We were our own United Nations, although no such institution yet existed, and the world would go through a global conflagration before it came into being.

Chapter 2
Diamonds and Arias

Regardless of their origins, a Jew feels "special" even at a young age. This knowledge may or may not be troublesome. One may feel blessed, as when we think of ourselves as a member of "The Chosen People," vulnerable, as when the Jewish community experiences antisemitism, or just different: so few of us, so many of them. Whatever the reason, there is a sense of uniqueness that comes with being a Jew.

A second reality of my young life added to my feeling different from other children. I was born with an infirmity; as I reached the age when one would toddle about, I didn't exactly toddle, more so, I hobbled. The reason for this? A "club" right foot, twisted from birth. In addition to their prayers, my parents sought a medical remedy for my condition, requiring two major surgeries and many awkward years in a leg brace. I was the object of both children's natural curiosity and derision. As I grew older and more self-conscious about it, I wore long pants even through the heat of our Dublin summers.

Being the son of the esteemed Chazzan Garb made me feel special in a good way. Da stood only five feet three inches, but his regal air and acute bearded visage impressed Jew and Gentile alike. I can still hear the deferential tones in the voices of people we'd meet during our walks. Jews would nod their head and wish my father a good day. When he inquired after their health, they would answer, "*Baruch Hashem.*" (Blessed is God.) This is how an Orthodox person

25

responds to this question, because after all, everything is in God's hands, including one's good health.

Rev. Wolf Garb, Manchester, England (1930)

"Top o' the morning, Father!" non-Jews jovially call out to him as they would a member of the Catholic clergy. More than once, I observed passers-by crossing themselves in his presence – the reason being that the garb worn by Jewish clergy is like that of a priest: a white collar over black cloth. My father responded to these misplaced greetings with understated politeness and courtesy. A quick nod and a fleeting smile communicated not only his good graces, but also his mild humor. In this way, he shielded himself as a Jew and an outsider. Meanwhile, I basked in the warmth of his prestige.

Often, these strange faces would look down at me and inquire, "And how are you, young man?" Before I could answer, Da's quick squeeze of my hand told me to smile and be quiet. Although outgoing today, I was, for many years, cautious and reserved in public, having learned well from my father.

Our first home was at 73 South Circular Road, Portobello, in the center of Dublin's tight-knit Jewish community. It was a short walk to the Greenville Hall Synagogue, where my father served as both cantor and bookkeeper. Ten years earlier, this area had witnessed some of the bloodiest combat of Ireland's civil war. To our Irish neighbors, those memories and wounds were still fresh. But for us who just arrived, the fighting might well have been ancient history.

Moving to Ireland had not improved my father's income. Indeed, the synagogue paid him only eight pounds a week, a pittance even then. "Oh, they pay you well, all right," my mother said, chiding him. "They pay you with respect and gratitude. Of course, you can't put food on your family's table with *that* now, can you?"

"We're doing fine," my father said. And he was being truthful; Da had kept his hand in the diamond trade, though with prudence.

The reason for his discretion lay in the wallets of the powerful synagogue council. Several of its members were well-established in Dublin's lucrative diamond trade and would not have looked kindly upon business being taken away from them by their very own cantor. When it came to feeding his family, such concerns were put aside. Many were the evenings my father sat in the dining room to work at his craft. Upon the well-polished table, he would set a black velvet cloth and spill out a pile of diamonds received from Grandpa Solomon in Antwerp.

"Do you see these?" he once asked, turning some glittering stones with a pair of tweezers. I came closer. "These are beautiful, flawless." I peered at the diamonds, but honestly, I could not tell one from another. "Which do you like best?" I pointed to the largest ones. He laughed. "Those are not nearly as valuable as these," he said, touching the smaller, more perfect stones.

A small, exact scale allowed him to weigh each of the stones with precision. Occasionally, a gentleman who came by to purchase diamonds took them at my father's word, without using the scale he had brought along as a double-check.

Da's pleasure was listening to music broadcast from Italy and other European countries on the Pilot wireless long-wave radio. On those evenings he was not engaged with diamonds, synagogue business, or one of his many charities, he would spread musical scores on the table and listen to his favorite operas, from Milan. Standing behind his chair, his eyes intent on the scores, his hands would conduct the performances from beginning to end, while he hummed along with the music.

As you can surely understand, our home was a musical one. If not my father tuning up for the coming Sabbath or polishing an aria while in the bath, it was Ma singing from one of Strauss' operettas in her pleasing soprano voice. As she sang, my father's tenor would wend itself around her voice in a harmonious accompaniment that Strauss had not envisioned but would surely have approved.

Aunt Jean, an operatic soprano, and Uncle David, a lyric tenor and cantor, fled Poland and came to live with us during the mid-1930s. At nineteen, Jean, the youngest of my father's siblings, entered a prestigious vocal competition called the "Irish Queen of Song." Women from throughout Ireland competed for this honor. During the pressure of the final rounds, she complained of a sore throat, and Da made his own special honey-tea remedy for her. Aunt Jean placed second, an achievement that delighted our
family, though there were murmurs of bias in the voting and that she truly deserved the title – but after all, for a Jewess to be crowned the *Irish* Queen of Song? Later on, during the war, she joined ENSA, the English equivalent of the USO, and sang for the British and American forces stationed in Belfast and London.

It seemed normal to be living among such amazing voices; they were a part of my everyday life. When a friend told of passing by and hearing a beautiful aria emanating from our window, I began to feel that we were players in a most unlikely opera. As children, our own musical training was taken as seriously as our religious studies. To my father and mother, each pursuit was an expression of the Divine.

Aunt Jean Garb "Eighteen"

Uncle David Garb & Wife, Freda (1940s)

When we observe the modern Orthodox Jewish community, we see religious Jews who enjoy the secular culture of today: the arts, sporting events, etc. Growing up, this was true for my family as well. We often frequented the opera at Dublin's Gaiety Theatre, where visiting companies from London and other European cities came to perform.

I cannot describe the thrill that I felt when, in the crowded and bustling opera house, after the curtain came down on the first act and intermission began, the pianist would ask if there was a performer in the audience who would sing from his or her seat. While most patrons headed for the restrooms or the bar, a devoted audience remained in their seats.

"Is Garb in the house?" My father waved to polite applause. Then the applause grew louder...

"Go on," mother would encourage him.

"Please, Da! Please?"

In the end, he always relented. Standing at his seat, he would perform one of his favorite arias: often "Celeste Aida" or the beautiful love duet from the first act of *La boheme*. When he finished, his face shining with perspiration, the hall echoed with bravos, and we huddled close to him, enchanted with our father, who could move an audience to such heightened applause.

* * *

Though an awfully busy man, Da was a guiding presence in the lives of his children, in particular, with myself and Abe. As his sons, he expected us to excel in our schooling, and he allowed no variance when it came to religious observance. As that famous fiddler on the roof asks generations of Jews: *How do we keep our balance? With tradition!*

Our traditions, handed down over centuries, have been codified into laws of observance and behavior, which all Jews are required to follow. And as the rabbis say, if all Jews are required to observe these laws, then *kal v'chomer* (how much more so) the responsibility is with those who lead the Jewish community. Rabbis and cantors are expected to be learned and observant exemplars. By extension, their entire households are to be models of Jewish life.

This placed an incredible burden on us, our father's children. After all, he chose to pursue a life of religious observance and leadership; we were born into it. The mantle did not always fit as you will come to learn later in my story.

In matters of observance, my father was a strict disciplinarian. While he was happy to engage us in rational discourse, in the end, the final word came from God; Hashem commands it, therefore, we are to do it. His desire was that we observe the commandments with a full heart.

"But why did Hashem forbid the eating of pork?" I once asked.

Da thought for a moment. "We Jews are very fortunate," he began, his eyes focused on me. "The Torah forbids the eating of any animal that does not have cloven hooves and that does not chew its cud. We don't often think about it, but pork is the source of many terrible illnesses, including trichinosis. By forbidding us pork, Hashem has saved us from disastrous health concerns."

For my father, God's commandments were a perfect marriage of Divine will and reason. If we felt restricted by them, he was sure that he could convince us of their merit through discussion. He took the time to do this with any of the commandments we questioned. Were my brother and I persuaded by Da's logic? More so as young children, but later on, we tended to do what our father wished out of obedience rather than fully embracing his devotion to God and Judaism.

There is no denying that as we grew to be teenagers, an anxiety festered within our hearts. The world called to us with its seductive powers, and we wanted nothing more than to answer that call. Judaism held us, while so much about Irish culture and society drew us into temptation. At times, the psychic clash between these two worlds was maddening. Children in many Orthodox families experienced the desire to rebel. Abey and I wrestled with this inner conflict as we followed the sometimes wayward paths of our lives.

Chapter 3

Manna from Heaven

The performance of *mitzvot,* or commandments, was the rule of our house and defined every aspect of our daily lives. *Remember the Sabbath day and keep it holy* is a commandment we fulfilled every week of the year. While I enjoyed Ma's cooking best on *Shabbos* (Sabbath), the holy day's restrictions annoyed me.

As you may know, one is not allowed to work on the Jewish Sabbath. But what does "to work" mean? To go to a job? Well, there's more to it. The ancient rabbis defined thirty-nine categories of work, but offered no precise definition. One such category is "kindling." Let me explain: you may notice observant Jews walking to shul on Sabbath mornings. In the rain or snow, the bitter cold or sweltering heat, they walk. It cannot be denied that it requires greater effort to walk than to drive, especially in inclement weather. But making fire was considered work and, in modern times, starting a car requires igniting the engine, so, no driving. They didn't distinguish among the various ways to create fire, whether by rubbing sticks together or, in this case, turning a key.

In today's world, rabbis ponder how to best honor age-old traditions in the face of modern technology. For example, they ruled that completing an electrical circuit, as in flipping a light or appliance switch, is equivalent to making fire. Hence, it is forbidden to turn on a light or operate machinery on the Sabbath. This is why religious Jews do not manually turn on lights or ovens, or drive, on Shabbos. One is allowed, however, to set a timer switch before sunset and have a well-lit home for Sabbath evening as well as turn on the oven or light a stove pilot flame, prior.

During winter months, with a choice between breaking a commandment or freezing, we, as most families in our community, hired a non-Jewish person to kindle our fire on the Sabbath. This "kindling" job was a respected vocation in Orthodox Jewish communities; people of distinction have had their first paying job as a *Shabbos Goy*. I seem to recall the actor James Cagney performed this service during his youth, on the Lower East Side of Manhattan.

What restrictions did the Sabbath place on me, the dutiful son of a cantor? Well, another definition of work, forbidden according to orthodoxy, is to carry anything on your person – certainly not money, which has no place in Sabbath observance. As a boy, I was so religious that I wouldn't carry even a handkerchief on Shabbos. I wore it in my sleeve so that it became a part of my clothing. You couldn't sport a watch either and, one day, I asked my father, "Why not? If wearing a handkerchief is okay, then surely a watch, no?" Da smiled, appreciating my logic, and then explained,

"A watch, Theo, is not made of simple cloth, but rather, metal. It is like a 'machine' with a mechanism that might require winding, lest you be tempted to do so on Shabbos."

Sabbath observance, like other aspects of my religious life, caused a gnawing anxiety to root in my soul. One incident that captures the unique conflict of being a Jew occurred soon after my Bar Mitzvah. I was having a walk late one Shabbos afternoon when, from the corner of my eye, I spotted what looked like a scrap of paper in the street. Coming closer, I realized it was money. A five-pound note! At that time, my father earned ten pounds a week – *this bill is half of Da's weekly wage!* You can imagine how my heart leapt.

I was caught in a terrible dilemma: if I picked up the note, I would be breaking the Sabbath. The thought of such a transgression had me in a nervous sweat, but to walk away from a huge sum of money was equally impossible. *What to do?* I'm sure King Solomon himself did not confront a problem more difficult than mine.

I've shared this incident with people over the years, and their response is that I should have asked a gentile passerby to place the note in my sleeve, wear it home, and reward them for helping me (after Shabbos of course!). Though I would be following Jewish law, it would not have been keeping with the spirit of it. And besides, that person might have kept it for themselves.

While sorting out my dilemma, the afternoon breeze teased the edge of the note, and now I had to worry about it blowing away, or worse – someone else taking it! I looked up and down the street and saw no one approaching, at least not yet. My whole body trembled as as I hit upon a plan. Taking one giant step off the sidewalk, I placed my right shoe over the note, and then, slowly, carefully, slid my foot back against the curb. And I stood there. . .

During this time, some of my friends walked by and invariably paused to exchange a few words with me.

"We're off to the park now. Come with us, Theo."

"No, I can't."

"Come on then. Why not?"

"I'm just going to stay here a while," I shrugged. They looked up and down the street.

"Stay here? What for?"

They teased me, suggesting that I was waiting on a girl, which I strongly denied. They accused me of being unfriendly. Others came and went, and then returned to see if I was still there. When they saw that I was, they began to think of it as a kind of game to convince me to move.

"What, are you doing a dare or something?"

"No, it's not a dare."

"What then?"

"I'm just standing here, that's all. I like it here." I smiled nervously, my eyes fixed on the pavement.

"Have you lost your mind?!"

"I'm thinking."

"Thinking?"

And so, I continued standing there. . . Standing and sitting, sitting and standing, my foot placed firmly over the note, my mind occupied with the happier memories of my recent Bar Mitzvah celebration, singing favorite songs and prayers to myself. Hours passed. . . In July, the sun doesn't set till after 9 p.m. in Ireland. It was approaching eight o'clock. Though my family often took naps on Shabbos afternoons and would expect me home for a late, light supper, by now, they must have been worried, *where is Theo?*

In the end, I was able to guard my secret treasure until it was *oys* Shabbos (end of Sabbath). How did I know? Look in the sky and, on a clear night, when you can count three stars at a glance, the Sabbath has ended. What a relief it was to reach down and pocket that five-pound note without fear of blemishing my immortal soul!

I arrived home and summoned the family to share my little adventure with them. Believe me, it was quite an animated retelling of standing in place for four hours. "And this is for you, Da," I beamed, placing the note in his hand. All smiles, he hugged me and said, "Good boy, Theo. That's using your *kop* (head)!"

Ma nodded her approval. "Theo, you're a clever boy! I always said so." That week, I was given an extra allowance – double my regular of two shillings and sixpence, which could buy a young lad quite a bit in those days.

Chapter 4
Rachel the *Baleboste*

Sabbath observance poses many challenges for Jews who live in the modern world and walk a tightrope between Jewish observance and secular life. Perhaps two or three hundred years ago in the *shtetls* (small Jewish towns), when the community was more insular, it was not so difficult. But today, the marvels of technology are tempting, and living an observant life is not so easy.

A way around the prohibition of lighting a fire on Shabbos is to prepare a stew that simmers from before the Sabbath begins until it is ready to be eaten on Saturday afternoon or evening. This stew, called *cholent,* was ambrosia for those who ate with us on a Shabbos afternoon. My mother was famous in the community for her cholent, many ingredients of which came from our garden. In addition to carrots and green vegetables, Ma's cholent consisted of a large stuffed *kishke* (derma), beef flanken, onions, barley, and plenty of potatoes. This wonderful dish was left to cook on a very low flame for twenty-four hours.

I was the gourmand in my family; whenever Ma cooked a meal, I'd be in the kitchen tasting everything. On these occasions, she would smile at me and pronounce, "Someday, Theo, you will be a chef on the Queen Mary!"

Funny that years later, I emigrated from Ireland to America aboard the Queen Mary. And it was on her worthy decks that I enjoyed, not cooking, but eating fine kosher meals, though not nearly as delicious as my mother prepared.

Well-known for her cooking and baking, Ma oversaw all domestic affairs; she was, what we call in Jewish, a *baleboste* (pron. balabusta). She did the laundry herself, even though we had a full-time sleep-in maid, Amy Morley, from Newcastle, England. Amy liked to remind us she hailed from "the city you never took coals to." (Listen for it: Cary Grant delivers a version of this line in *Philadelphia Story*.)

In those days, laundering was not merely the task of sorting and placing clothes in a washer with a cup of detergent. Washing clothes meant scrubbing them by hand on a washboard in the bathtub. They were then brought outside and hung to dry. This was no small task, especially with so many of us to care for. After a long day of cooking and chores, Ma would spend her evenings in the parlor, embroidering on fine Irish linens, while singing along with Da.

Like many families in our neighborhood, we actively tended our fruit and vegetable garden. During World War II, these were called "Victory Gardens." Da started ours soon after we moved to our second house in 1941, which had a large backyard. In addition to lettuce, tomatoes, string beans, peas, radishes, potatoes, and other vegetables, we planted an orchard of apple trees. If you visit, you'll see they bear fruit, even today.

One old pear tree bore hundreds of delicious pears each season. Our next-door neighbor, Mr. Gunne, had a friend who owned a canning factory, and that gentleman canned our surplus pears so they lasted well into the next year or two. We also kept chickens, everyone did. What would Shabbos be without fresh chickens?

Chapter 5
A Visit with the Shochet

For our family, having a chicken ready for the Sabbath meal involved much more than going to a kosher butcher and purchasing one. I remember the first time Ma gave me the responsibility of bringing a chicken to the shochet; I couldn't have been more than twelve. Until then, I had only collected the eggs from chickens, but this day would be different.

In the morning, I was assigned the job of catching two chickens and bringing them to the slaughterhouse on Clanbrassil Street. I called across the yard to my friend, Shloime, and he ran over to help. Together, we tiptoed into the garden and set down the wicker basket that would carry the chickens to market. At first, the task was like a game of tag for us. We chased after them as they squawked and scrambled out of reach.

"Hey, over here!" I cried out, grasping one by the neck, only to have it squirm loose.

"You have to grab their legs!" Shloime shouted.

"What makes you the expert on catching chickens? You haven't caught one yet."

"I'm just having fun. You're the one who has to do the catching."

"Great."

"And I've watched mum do it lots of times, so I know what's to be done."

"Then help me!" I snapped, frustrated with him.

We soon chased down two chickens, and, as Shloime held one and then the other, I wrapped their legs with twine and plopped them into the wicker basket. "There, it's done," I said triumphantly, wiping the sweat off my brow. "Come on!"

We walked along Clanbrassil Street, or "Little Jerusalem" as it was known, the basket kicking and swinging between us. Even if you've never been to Dublin, you may know of this street. In James Joyce's *Ulysses*, Leopold Bloom is likened to Homer's wandering hero, Ulysses, because as a Jew – and an Irish Jew at that – he wanders throughout Dublin in search of his true identity. Joyce mentions number 52 Upper Clanbrassil Street, and there is a plaque on the door informing us that this house is where Leopold Bloom was born and lived with his wife, Molly.

Clanbrassil Street was filled with Jewish shops. There were several kosher butchers: Rubenstein's, Ehrlich's, Abe Samuel's (with his partner, Mr. Walzman), Smully Davis', and Goldwater's. Mr. Atkins had a shoe repair store, and Mr. Wertzburger, a cigarette shop. There was a Jewish bookstore, a Judaica shop, and kosher wines and spirits. Becky Daniels owned a drapery shop. Mrs. Fine and Barney Davis each ran a grocery store. Ordman's Delicatessen offered cold cuts and large barrels of pickled and *schmaltz* herrings.

There was never the fear of having a Jewish name displayed in large letters on a storefront; this was wonderful and not taken for granted by the community. That sense of security was remarkable considering Jewish history in other lands and what was about to take place in Europe.

We carried the basket to Rev. Moher, a man who, for a few pence, slaughtered all sorts of fowl. "What've we here, boys?" he asked, wiping his hands on his apron as we approached.

"Two chickens for Shabbos," I said.

"Hello, Theo, how are your parents? Please wish them a good Shabbos for me."

"I will, Rev. Moher, and a good Shabbos to you." Shloime and I lifted the basket onto the table.

"They look like nice birds," he said, eyeing them closely. "Of course, we won't know for sure until they're plucked."

Plucking, however, was not Rev. Moher's responsibility. He took one chicken at a time into his arms, holding it tightly around and, with a razor-sharp blade, slit its throat. He then placed the birds upside-down in a cone-shaped funnel, so the blood could drain.

Now, there are kosher and *treif* (non-kosher) animals. Those that are treif cannot be eaten under any circumstances. To be kosher, an animal must be slaughtered and prepared in a prescribed manner. The first thing is, they must be killed as humanely as possible. That is why a chicken's throat is swiftly cut, rather than snapping its neck or clubbing the animal. Another requirement is to fully drain its blood.

When this ritual slaughter was completed, Rev. Moher told us to visit the next room where the chicken flickers sat in sauna-like heat. We entered and observed women seated on low benches with chickens, ducks, and geese in their laps. A pungent smell of fresh blood, sweat, and raw flesh filled the air – it was nauseating. I nearly vomited but held back, taking in shallow breaths through my mouth.

The women chatted and laughed as they plucked our birds to the last feather. These feathers were valuable and carefully separated to be used in the making of pillows and blankets. After several minutes, they handed us our bald and lifeless chickens, and we placed them gently into the basket.

"A *guten* Shabbos!" said the women, smiling.

The sun waned. . . The Sabbath was near as Shloime and I arrived home. Ma greeted us at the door and asked how our mission went.

"The plucking room smelled terrible!" I said.

She shrugged and said, "It's hard work plucking chickens all day in a closed room." I remember her dour expression that told me she felt fortunate not to be one of those women.

Ma placed each chicken on a board blanketed with coarse salt. This was to draw any remaining blood from the animal's flesh. It didn't matter what kind of meat it was – chicken, steak, liver, whatever – it was salted so that all the blood was drawn from it. She salted both chickens for more than an hour before inspecting every inch of their flesh, while making small clucking sounds with her tongue.

As she examined the second chicken, I could tell from her facial expressions that she was concerned. "Come, I want you to take this bird to Rabbi Alony, and ask him what he thinks."

You see, in addition to everything else, for meat to be kosher, it must be unblemished. If there's a stain of any kind, a rabbi determines if this mark renders the animal unkosher. Rabbis were the authority in this analysis; they even specialized in different animals.

I rode my bicycle to the rabbi's home, not far from ours, to *pasken a shaila* (ask a question). The rabbi greeted me warmly and scrutinized the chicken with care; he ruled that the bird was kosher. If he had declared otherwise, it could either be sold or given away to a non-Jewish person.

My mother was relieved to hear the good news, as we were having guests for Sabbath dinner, and it was important to have two chickens to serve so there would be plenty for everyone.

Chapter 6

Matzah Biscuits? Woof!

While keeping a kosher home is not an easy task, it is less troublesome than keeping kosher for *Pesach* (Passover), especially in Dublin that year. A kosher home for Pesach means performing a deep cleansing of your house: sweeping, mopping, and vacuuming floors; cleaning cabinets, counters, appliances, ovens, and stovetops, with soap and water; *kashering* (making kosher) the silverware, glassware, and dishes by immersing them in large pots of boiling water, with a stone placed inside (to help maintain water temperature as more items are added).

Another requirement is *mechiras chometz* (the selling of leavened foods). Any food in your home deemed unkosher for Passover is "sold" to a non-Jew by your community's rabbi, for the duration of the festival. The food remains in your possession, stored away, and the family usually buys it back after the holiday.

Then the search for and burning of chometz takes place – even the smallest crumb, from a piece of bread, cookie, cracker, or cake, that may be hiding under a couch, the oven, the fridge. There can be absolutely no chometz in your possession during the eight days of Passover.

As you may know, Jews eat matzah rather than bread on Pesach to symbolize the haste with which our ancestors left Egypt. Irish Jews were no exception to this edict of tradition. Our supply of matzah was usually shipped over from England, but during the war, shipping was interrupted by the dangers posed by German U-boats and the havoc caused by the Battle of Britain. While Ireland was somewhat isolated by its geography and neutral politics, its Jewish community would have been hard-pressed to observe Pesach without matzah.

Aware of the looming threat, our religious leaders searched for a local factory where they could manufacture kosher matzah. With a global war raging across continents, their plan would take time to implement. Kosher matzah requires special dough and the baking equipment must be thoroughly kashered – not an overnight process. In the end, community leaders located a factory in Dublin – Spratt's, which manufactured dog biscuits – and asked if they would allow the Jewish community to use part of the factory for baking matzah.

This required that a section of the plant be shut down and made kosher for Passover, the matzah baked, and the factory promptly returned to the making of dog biscuits. Dublin's Jewish leaders would also need to provide matzah for the Jews of Cork, Limerick, and elsewhere; that translated into thousands of pounds of it. After some negotiation, the deal was finalized, and the Jewish community was set to bake 'round the clock in early spring of 1940.

Rabbis and bakers were summoned to assist in blessing and preparing the dough: kosher flour and a little water – that was it. As tradition instructs, it was baked for no more than eighteen minutes from the time the flour and water were mixed.

The entire endeavor, though well-intentioned, was a catastrophe! For one, the equipment was tooled for dog biscuits, which were four-by-two inches, while matzah is usually seven-by-seven-inch squares. Now, there is no law regarding the size or shape of matzah, but this was an odd thing for everyone, and it was the least of the problems.

All the matzah produced at the factory, the thousands of pounds of matzah baked for the entire Jewish population of Ireland that year, turned out to be as hard as a rock! Anyone with false teeth had no hope of biting into it, and those of us with real teeth stood the risk of breaking them – how disappointing. Every year, I looked forward to a piece of matzah with a shmear of cream cheese or butter, topped with thick-cut marmalade, for a snack. Sadly, as I recall, there was one recorded fatality: a dog fed these matzah biscuits died of a blocked stomach.

The only way this matzah was edible for man or beast was to soak it in warm water for a long time, longer than usual, and make "matzah brei," a favorite breakfast of mine during Passover. Matzah brei consists of broken pieces of matzah mixed with eggs and milk, and then fried like pancakes. A little jam or maple syrup on the side, it makes for a hearty and delicious meal. I'll tell you, there was a glut of matzah brei consumed in Ireland that year!

Who said Spratts?
SPRATT'S
Meat Fibrine
Dog Cakes
FOR
HEALTH, ENERGY & STAMINA.

Chapter 7

My First Day at School

But I have strayed from my story. In addition to keeping a kosher home, schooling was an important issue confronting the Irish Jewish community. After all, without Jewish schools, how could the next generation be properly taught the laws and traditions of Judaism? Unfortunately, there were no Jewish day schools in Ireland, so I had little choice but to attend a Presbyterian school. It was either that or a Catholic school, which was a far less desirable choice since the Catechism was central to their teachings.

My secular education began at the Donore Terrace School, located in a Presbyterian church nearby; I attended for two years. That first day of school I remember as if it were yesterday. I can still feel the reassuring grasp of my mother's hand as we walked together the fifteen minutes from our house to the church; I was all of three years and two months old. This day was especially strange in that I had never before interacted with non-Jewish children. My only contact with them had been in shops with my mother, or on the street with my father. In my experience, the entire world was Jewish. And so, when my mother said goodbye, I had little understanding that I was about to enter a new world – a world shared with children of a different faith.

In Dublin, even among Orthodox families, we children dressed like other Irish children. That is, we weren't identifiable by our clothing. And yet, on that first day of school, when I encountered more new faces than ever before, it happened that those I became friendly with were also Jewish. It was as though an inner voice had called upon us to seek and find each other.

My first day of school was memorable for another reason; vivid in my recollection are the events of that night. As any youngster, I was instinctively in tune with the adult moods and sensitivities around me, knowing when something was bothering mother or father, even as they tried to hide it: a certain look in their eyes, a slight tremor in the hand that held mine, or an edge in my father's voice when he gave instructions. That evening, the usual light ambience was shattered by an intrusion from the outside world that would change us all, forever.

We sat in the living room after dinner, and I remember the light from the radio reflecting in my father's eyes as he studied the dial, trying to pinpoint the station he desired. Remember, technology then was not what it is today; tuning into a station was challenging.

He soon became frustrated with his attempt. "Where have they hidden it this evening?" he said, as he continued making small adjustments on the dial, with greater and lesser waves of static emanating from the speakers. I could feel the electricity in the room, a tension that had less to do with his finding the station than with something else that I could yet understand. Ma sat stiffly upright in her chair, watching my father, her face distorted by shadows and an unspoken fear. "Perhaps they're not broadcasting tonight," she said.

My father did not look up at her and responded in a huff, "Ridiculous! They must broadcast." There was gravity in his voice that I thought was odd. "I will find it," he insisted. Thinking back to this early childhood memory, I realize it wasn't music Da was searching for.

Pilot Wireless Radio (1930s)

Several long minutes ensued. Then, as if hurled from the static, a remarkably clear voice spoke, a voice unlike any I'd ever heard, in a language foreign to me. There was a chilling quality to it, a relentless droning tenor that made me shiver with fear.

As the broadcast continued, my father's expression froze with rage. I sensed he wanted nothing more than to turn the dial and close our home to the sound of that voice. But he was unable to act. It was as if a *dybbuk* (devil) had entered our home and rendered us all powerless. Hypnotic and drenched with emotion, the cadence of this voice rose and fell. Ma's lips parted slightly and her eyes widened – she looked terrified. I watched Da's fist clench and unclench. *What's happening? What is the voice saying?* I wanted to know, but in my fear and confusion, I was paralyzed to ask.

Then, an eerie silence. . . The voice of Adolf Hitler had blared through the wireless, filling our hearts with fear and anger. No music played in the Garb home that evening – none. The dybbuk was out and alive in the world. Who would he visit next?

Hitler's bullying came as no surprise to my father. This was

1932, and for years, Da had viewed the political changes in Germany with concern. My father was not innocent in his understanding of the world. He did not flinch at the horrors that lay ahead. But like others who guessed what was to come, he did not have the power to change the fate of humankind.

Chapter 8
Seeking Refuge

An ardent Zionist, Rev. Wolf Garb had recently been appointed secretary to the Dublin branch of the World Zionist Organization. I surmise this was the outcome of a visit to Dublin by Dr. Nahum Sokolow, its president, in the spring of 1933. Among Da's correspondence is a letter from Rabbi Herzog dated May 5th of that year, an invitation to welcome Dr. Sokolow to Dublin the following week, in the boardroom of the Central Hotel on Exchequer Street. Dr. Herzog concluded with a request for my mother's and father's "valuable advice and co-operation."

Of course, they were delighted to oblige. With his heart and soul, Da believed that one day there would be a State of Israel, a Jewish homeland, to end our two thousand years of wandering. In the meantime, he was a pragmatist who thought that Ireland could serve as a Jewish haven and an avenue of escape from Hitler's evil grasp for members of our family.

Driven by a sense of urgency, my parents began to correspond with them and journey abroad with a single aim: to bring their families from Poland and Belgium to Ireland – efforts that were to have a dramatic effect on my early life. The size of our household would increase, year by year, until there were nine of us, not including the temporary lodgers, whom they welcomed with hospitality worthy of our ancestors, Abraham and Sarah.

With the help of many who were sympathetic to the cause, including then member of Parliament, Robert Briscoe, my father was able to secure passage and eventual approval from the Irish immigration authorities for his father, Shlomo, to emigrate from Poland in January 1934. The next year, my father's brother, David, and their sister, Jean, followed. The addition of Aunt Jean and Uncle David to our household was especially grand; their ascending harmonies would bring a measure of comfort and warmth to our home when it was most needed. Two other siblings, Aron and Leon, and their wives and children, chose to remain in Warsaw, unaware of the dangers ahead. . .

Other than the birth of my sister, Sarah, those pre-war times offered less and less to sing about. No other family members responded to my father's pleas for them to come to Ireland. "Why can't they see?!" he cried out many times in frustration.

What was obvious to us seemed veiled to those who were about to experience the most brutal atrocities in history. Polish Jews accounted for nearly a third of the population of Warsaw and ten percent of Poland's population overall, living relatively peaceful lives there for centuries. Religious Jews touted it as a *Gan Eden* (Garden of Eden) for the Jewish people. But as the situation in Poland grew ominous, the hardships more real, Polish Jews lived in denial of their fate.

Our dining table continued to grow through those years, as well as the many dialects spoken around it. English and Yiddish were the first languages of our household. When my *zeyde* (grandfather) came over from Warsaw, more Yiddish was spoken. Over time, English, Yiddish, Polish, Russian, and a smattering of Hebrew flew back and forth, especially Yiddish, when topics not suitable for children's ears were being discussed. We learned quickly though, and Yiddish became our second tongue.

In addition to our family, we had a number of lodgers rooming with us. Many were single Jewish men who were refugees before and during the war and who worked in Dublin. They paid for their food and lodging and often told grim tales of life in their towns and villages in Eastern Europe before they fled; none of their talk was hopeful. To this day, when I try to sort out all the people who stayed with us, I cannot fathom where they slept. How we managed was nothing short of a miracle.

I remember a time that I went with my mother to answer a knock on our front door...

"Yes?" she inquired to a slight, wide-eyed young man standing in the doorway, furtively glancing over his shoulder.

"Hello, ma'am," he said. "I understand you take in lodgers."

With that, Rodney came into our home and lived with us for the duration of the war. Soon enough, we discovered he was not the usual lodger. He was a "fly boy" draft dodger from England, who had no money and never worked. As I recall, he rarely left the house except at night, and then only briefly. I would come to understand the reason for his secrecy: English officers were on the lookout for deserters, who, if captured, would be court-martialed and imprisoned, if not hung.

Apart from the stray deserter and handful of rescued family members, there was a constant stream of young Jewish men in our home – rabbis, students, and laymen – all looking for work in the Jewish community, traumatized by the terrors they had fled. My mother was heartbroken that her own father, Solomon Rosenstrauch, resisted her pleas to bring the family out of Belgium. Perhaps his wealth and standing as a prosperous diamond merchant, jeweler and friend to the royal families of Europe, blinded him to the fact that, in the eyes of the evil to come, he was simply a Jew: a Jew whose material riches could not save him, his wife, Taube, their son, Henrik (my "Uncle Harry"), nor any other family member, from the coming storm.

Da's efforts may have been futile, but he could not remain silent in the face of that evil. Indeed, he took a stand whenever and wherever possible. In January 1938, he wrote a fierce letter to the newly appointed German ambassador to Ireland, Eduard Hempel, which read in part:

> You have robbed the Jews of their possessions, and you are still robbing them every day. Your end is coming as is the end of Hitler's gang. The hangman is near, much nearer than you think. Get in touch with your Fuehrer to stop this murder. The Jews are helpless and go like sheep to the slaughter. Don't start your dirty tricks here in this peaceful country with your propaganda. There is no room here for your kind. The sooner you go the better. Do you know how you are hated by all 75 million true Germans in Germany and Germans all over the world?

There is no indication that my father ever heard back from the German ambassador. Still, we can guess that Rev. Garb's highly visible profile and his activities in support of the Jewish community rendered him a mark for Hitler's gang of Nazis. Although he predicted an end to their evil-doing, it came too late for millions of

European Jews and Polish Catholics, among others, as the German war machine trampled on humanity in the years ahead.

TELEPHONE:
AVENUE 5377.

OFFICE OF THE CHIEF RABBI

4, CREECHURCH PLACE, ALDGATE,

LONDON, E.C.3.

4th April, 1940.

Dear Mr. Garb,

    Thousands of destitute Polish Jewish Refugees and War Victims now stranded in Lithuania, Roumania and other places in Eastern Europe are beseeching us for Matzos for Passover. Their sufferings are indescribable and the approach of the sacred Festival has intensified their anguish and despair.

    We are appealing to you to help us to provide Matzos and other Passover necessities for these hapless exiles. We are confident that every Jew will promptly respond to our urgent call. Time is short. Our relief must reach the local Refugee Committees well before the Seder-Nights.

    Please make a thank-offering because you and your dear ones have escaped the miseries of our afflicted Polish Refugee brethren.

    May the God of our Fathers bless all those who will extend help generously and immediately. May He speedily cause the Passover of Freedom to dawn for the whole House of Israel.

Sincerely Yours,

J. H. Hertz
Chief Rabbi.

I. Abramsky
Dayan.

Harris M. Lazarus
Dayan.

Letter to Rev. Wolf Garb from the Chief Rabbi of England, Rabbi J. H. Hertz, Dated April 4, 1940

Excerpt: Thousands of destitute Polish Jewish refugees and war victims now stranded in Lithuania, Romania, and other places in Eastern Europe are beseeching us for matzos for Passover. Their sufferings are indescribable, and the approach of the sacred festival has intensified their anguish and despair...

Chapter 9

The Long Shadows of War

As a boy, I was captured by the images on postage stamps, which arrived in our home through my father's correspondence with family and business associates abroad. I started a collection and became aware of world leaders, famous and important people, and world geography. Stamps and school were my tools of learning. In 1934, Rabbi Herzog determined that it was time for the Jewish community to have its own elementary school, and so, my tenure at the Presbyterian school ended. No doubt the events in Europe as well as an emerging Jewish identity defined by Zionism prompted his decision.

With the support of Jewish philanthropists and the Irish government, the necessary funds were raised and, in a very short time, Zion Schools was built. Curiously, its teachers and principal were non-Jews – Catholics and Protestants – who taught our secular subjects: math, science, history, English, French and Latin. At three o'clock, we went home to have a cup of tea and do our school work and returned at either 4 p.m. or 6 p.m. for Hebrew School. Hebrew classes were five days a week, two hours a day, from Sunday through Thursday. Saturday, the Sabbath, was a day for prayer and a well-deserved rest. Every subject relevant to Israel and Judaism was taught: reading, writing, and speaking Hebrew, Jewish history, Jewish holidays, prayer, and Torah study. After sixth grade, we attended Protestant schools until university.

*Zion Schools, Dublin (1941), Theo Pictured in Middle Row,
2nd from Right (Shloime behind him)*

School dominated my life, and our household routine began early, since Da was obliged to attend the eight o'clock morning *minyan* (communal prayer service), six days a week. The weekday minyan was only half an hour, while the Shabbat morning service, as today, was three hours long. During the week, we would sit together as a family for breakfast. Ma served us porridge, soft-boiled eggs, tea, and fabulous Irish breads: turnover, malt, soda bread, and rye. We brought bagged lunches to school, and supper at home was often a nourishing meal of fish, eggs, and potatoes. Of all the dishes Ma prepared, my favorite was fried plaice. It was similar to flounder, and she served it with a lettuce and tomato salad, and whole potatoes roasted over coals.

But no weekday meal could measure up to the Sabbath's for sheer culinary delight. We came home after morning services and an *oneg* (a light meal) at the shul and rested. Then we played in the garden, awaiting the *Shalosh Seudos,* the "Third Feast" of Shabbos, with Ma's cholent, the highlight of this feast. Long ago, the rabbis determined that the Sabbath was a day when every Jew, no matter their station in life, should feel like royalty. On the Sabbath, we displayed our finery, not to impress others but, rather, to thank God for His many blessings – blessings that were soon overshadowed by events unfolding abroad.

My parents' greatest fears came to pass, when, on September 1, 1939, Hitler's army invaded Poland; then in May 1940, the Nazi juggernaut advanced into Belgium. And like a spigot turned off, the flow of letters and diamonds came to a halt. My father redoubled his efforts to send food and clothing to family and others in the besieged Jewish communities of Eastern and Central Europe. However, we never knew for sure these items reached those in need.

Our home had always possessed a spirit of music hopeful for a better tomorrow. But now, a dissonant chord entered, and heaviness clung to everything. I was ten years old and aware of the changes in my world. Abey, fifteen, asked my father how God could allow these terrible things to happen to the Jews.

"I don't know," my father shook his head.

"Where's the redemption?" Abe asked, pressing him.

"When we will have a homeland," Da said. "We must have a place that is ours. The world is not kind to us."

"Not kind?" Abe sneered.

"God will provide an answer."

"And if God doesn't, will we?"

With such discourse taking place, and with refugees arriving from European cities, sharing their tales of Hitler's brutal and relentless march, there was no escaping the truths of the outside world. As a boy, I had no perspective with which to understand these harsh realities – realities that would later define me as a person, an Irishman, and a Jew. Ireland's declaration of neutrality in the war meant that my family would be safe, even as our European Jewish brethren faced increasing dangers and hardships. I took pride and solace in being Irish. However, the Jewish side of me was in turmoil.

Anguished expressions were etched in the faces of my parents and those who came to visit. Day after day, I sensed my mother's fear as she prayed for the well-being of her relatives. Faith sustained us, but God seemed distant.

Rachel & Wolf (1939)

The radio, with both a physical and psychic presence, that magically brought music into our home over the years, was now tuned to a continual stream of dire news, which poured into the living room.

As the adults collapsed onto our sofa and chairs, I was often asked to tune the Pilot wireless in search of the latest news.

My Dad taped a large map of Europe to the kitchen wall and tracked the advancing German war machine. Colored pins marked its battles and the retreats of the armies it faced. Each week, there were more and more pins, and I felt the war draw closer to our Irish homeland. At times, I was desperate to escape the worry that permeated the very fabric of our lives. The enemy had infiltrated our hearts and souls, waging battle within us.

Still, we enjoyed small victories. One was the steady growth of the Zionist movement after the first waves of Jewish émigrés entered British-controlled Palestine. As the Brits tried to suppress this migration, the Irish, who had suffered centuries of British domination, now cheered our cause. Irish support for the Zionist mandate traced back to the previous decade, when British courts hanged the first Jewish émigré for engaging in violent protest. Irish Catholics and Jews responded with a single voice; people who have known oppression cry out from the same soul. The rising tide of anti-British sentiment in the early war years is what encouraged my parents to hide the British fly-boy.

Ireland's neutrality afforded many benefits for its citizens, not least of which was creating interludes of relative calm in a world gone mad. While there were shortages of petrol, tea, coffee, sugar, butter, cigarettes, and the like, we never went hungry; there was plenty of food. The Irish even shipped cattle, sheep, fowl, and eggs to England to nourish their war effort. Our coupon-filled ration books reminded us of war's daily sacrifice. In the same time, Ireland provided its citizens with a degree of sanctuary not found in many other countries.

Despite the war's rationings, my parents managed to provide a comfortable life for our family.

Strange as it seems, I remember happy times during those years. After all, I was a young boy with a world to conquer. As my understanding of the plight of European Jewry grew, there were moments of youth's innocence that glitter in my memory still.

* * *

Our family's custom was to make summer retreats to a charming seaside resort at Bray, in County Wicklow, an hour's drive south of Dublin. One could walk along the promenade there and follow a road that spiraled up toward the summit, known as Bray Head, which towered above the coast. The path was wide and smooth, with grass and flowers growing on either side. There were plateaus along the route where shops and cafés stood, allowing visitors to relax and spend a few pence as well. Vacationers who made their way to the top were rewarded with a restaurant and bar called the Eagle's Nest. I can still see my mother and father standing at an observation railing nearby, looking out over the emerald countryside and glistening sea.

"I love it here," ma whispered. My father didn't answer; the look of calm on his face said everything.

It was an arduous hike to the top for parents with young children. And yet, the view of the countryside, and the sea so far below that it was impossible to hear the waves crashing on the shore, made the climb more than worth it. For a young boy, the entire world seemed visible. I gazed in all directions, straining my eyes to see as far as the ends of the Earth.

The memories of Bray Head are with me today: the serene look on my parents' faces, the caress of the sea breeze, the excitement of people arriving at the summit for the first time, the cooking smells of the Eagle's Nest, and the emotions welling up inside me – memories that fill me with the wonder of my youth. Closing my eyes, I can feel the sea breeze on my face, still. I cherished those long walks to the summit despite my leg brace that added a few extra pounds.

"Are you sure you want to keep going?" Ma would ask. Determined, I'd nod my head and press on. Along the way, we often met up with people we knew or who recognized my father from Greenville Hall. It was no accident that Bray was referred to as "Little Jerusalem." Because of the need to maintain the dietary laws of kashrus, it can be difficult at times for religious people to travel. A limited number of places in Dublin served kosher meals; Stein's Hotel on Harrington Street and the Hotel Lawrence on Harcourt Street were two. For the most part, we ate in our homes or the homes of other Jewish families.

Occasionally, we would have tea and dessert in one of the fabulous cafés of Dublin: Bewley's or Roberts' Café on Grafton Street, or Switzer's Café, located in a grand department store on Wicklow Street. Students from Trinity College and other universities frequented these cafés, where they engaged in animated discussions about world events, politics, and literature. They also went there to meet girls. To this day, I can savor the taste of my favorite cream puffs; their cakes and pastries were legendary!

With eating establishments for Jews so limited, Bray offered lodging and kosher meals, which made it all the more an attractive vacation spot. It felt like home, and we enjoyed our bungalow there for a number of years. At some point, my father thought it would be a pleasant change to vacation away from the community where he lived and worked. In 1941, he and my mother found a quieter, more relaxing venue.

"Why do we have to go somewhere else?" I asked, disappointed.

"Your father feels it's best," Ma said, though not to my satisfaction. Da always had the last word, and there was nothing more to say.

So it was that we began to vacation in Wicklow Town, a resort farther south from Dublin than Bray, on the Irish Sea. For the duration of the war, a bungalow there would be our summer home.

Chapter 10
Hitler's Synagogue

In January 1941, we looked forward to moving to a larger house at 97 Donore Terrace, just opposite the Greenville Hall Synagogue. Everything was packed away and ready for the move, when, on the night of January 2nd – the sound of approaching aircraft. . . Until this moment, Ireland's neutrality had protected her from the violence of war. Daily life was void of the fear that people experienced in England and the rest of Europe. All of that changed with the roar of fighters in the skies above.

I awoke from my sleep, startled by the growing roar of the planes. I ran downstairs and saw my father standing in the living room, his neck, craned, his ear pointed skyward.

"What's that noise?" I asked.

Da shot a glance in my direction. "Shhh."

His hearing, so brilliantly attuned to music, was now like radar searching to identify another sound.

"My God," Ma whispered under her breath.

We children could sense her fear as she gathered us close. We all looked to my father, silently asking for guidance. The noise of the planes became deafening, as to be a physical presence – the very air shook. The sensation was so powerful, I remember thinking they were going to land on our house! As Luftwaffe fighters soared above, the pilots loosed their bombs into the night sky. . . boom! boom!! boom!!! A thunderous trio of explosions sounded – we screamed and clung to one another, as the earth trembled. . .

The noise of the airplanes receded into the distance. We dressed quickly and hurried outside. The bombs had landed in the vicinity of Greenville Hall. We ran to the area... and could not believe our eyes!

Sirens filled the night air, heading toward us. Neighbors lit torches and made their way through the darkness. Torch flames and burning roofs' fiery embers made a silhouette of everyone, against the cold, dark night. I hid behind Da, frightened to look, but compelled to see. I will never forget the strange shadows cast upon the worried faces of our friends and neighbors by the glowing light.

People were shouting names all over the area: "Where is Revered Roith? Has anyone seen the Roith family?"

"Are the Caseys all right?"

"Is the Marcus family injured?"

The night air was filled with panicked cries for the several families who lived in the bombed houses. The crowd pushed forward toward the burning homes, determined to save anyone they could. Just then, firemen and ambulances arrived. A few ARP (Air Raid Precautions) personnel from the neighborhood volunteered to help.

"Anyone hurt?" a fireman called out. No one knew. "How many people in this house?" he asked, pointing to the Roith home.

My father informed him the number of people in the Roith family. Looking at the rubble, the fireman took the news with a grim expression. The Roith house took a direct hit and was practically demolished. I trembled with fear and cold as this exchange took place. He looked at my father and about to speak, he stopped, turned, and entered the house.

Da gathered men from the neighborhood, enough to form a minyan, and chanted a *mish'berach,* a prayer of healing, in a soft, quivering voice. I never heard my father chant so softly and so poignantly before.

Will they be back? This was everyone's silent fear.

Suddenly, a joyous cry! We looked to the Roith home, and there, being carried from the wreckage, was Reverend Roith, his wife, and his children. They were bloodied and in pain but survived a range of injuries that would take months to heal. A miracle had occurred – all were alive. Not one person, from the homes destroyed, was killed. Baruch Hashem!

I believe that God was looking over Dublin's Irish and Jewish communities that night. My father hurried over to the reverend minister being placed gently into the ambulance. I didn't hear the conversation, but their somber and determined expressions spoke volumes to me.

"The synagogue's been hit!" the sextant cried. Our hearts fell. For a moment, there was silence, and then my father led us across the road. Shrapnel from the bombs had defaced the building's stone facade. Inside, the *Beis Hamidrash* (mini-chapel), reserved for weekday prayer, lay in a shambles of splintered furniture and shattered glass. Repairs to Greenville Hall were made as quickly as possible. For a while though, our hearts remained deeply bruised by this violation of God's holy temple.

After the incident, both the Irish and Jewish papers were filled with news of the bombing. Greenville Hall became known as "Hitler's Synagogue," as there was a chilling suspicion that the Luftwaffe intended to destroy it. Since Ireland had declared neutrality in the war, Greenville Hall was the only synagogue in Europe that Germany was ordered to pay reparations for. In the coming months, there were to be more Dublin bombings and air strikes in other counties of Ireland as well.

THE IRISH TIMES, SATURDAY, JANUARY 4, 1941.

AFTER DUBLIN BOMBING

WRECKED HOUSES in Donore terrace, and (right) removing clothing from one of them.

IIEVING household articles (above), and (below) some salvaged property.

Bottom Right: Greenville Hall Synagogue's Weekday Mini-Chapel in Shambles

The Irish Times, Saturday, January 4, 1941

Excerpt: Fragments of the explosive and incendiary bombs dropped. . . have been examined and found to be of German origin. In response, an Associated Press message from Berlin states: "These bombs are English, or they are imaginary. Our flyers have not been over Ireland and have not been sent there, so someone else will have to explain those bombs."

In the hysteria of this attack, I almost forgot that we would be moving directly across from the Greenville Hall Synagogue and two doors away from the Roith family. Our future home was also damaged – a part of the roof and the brick wall of my bedroom, wrecked by shrapnel.

I was having nightmares about the move: German fighter planes returning to finish their destruction of the synagogue, and I didn't want to be living across the street when they did!

"Don't worry," my mother said. "They're not coming back. It was a mistake."

"Why, because Hitler said so? I don't want to move!"

"It will be all right." And so, we moved into our new home in the spring, after the roof and other structural damages were repaired.

At this point, no one doubted Germany's ability to wreak havoc, even in a neutral country. Later that year, a German land mine exploded in the North Strand area of Dublin, killing twenty-eight people and leaving nearly 400 homeless.

But that was in the future, and the bombing, in the past. By the summer of 1941, there were more important things for a young Jewish, Irish lad to be worried about – namely, my Bar Mitzvah, just a year away. Before school and Bar Mitzvah studies in September, our family drove south along the coast and arrived in Wicklow Town for the summer holidays.

Chapter 11
A Cottage by the Sea

There were but two other Jewish families in Wicklow. Professor Weidman, a widower who lived alone, taught violin to the local children. In his youth, he played the violin in the Palm Court of a famous London hotel. However, it was, as he said, "in another lifetime." The other Jewish family was that of Bernard "Barney" Shillman, a famous barrister. Known in the Jewish community for a book he wrote in 1945, titled *A Short History of the Jews in Ireland*, to the Irish, he was a legal expert who specialized in Labor Law and Workman's Compensation. His books on those subjects are studied even today. He and my father became close friends during our vacations in Wicklow.

It was years later I discovered how far Da's friendship with Barney Shillman extended, when I came upon a score card from the Wicklow Golf Club with my father's and Barney Shillman's names on it. I was amazed, as I could not picture my dad as a golfer. When I asked my siblings if they'd known of his golf outings, they expressed the same disbelief. It shows you how little children know about their parents.

Golf seemed so un-Jewish in those days. To me, Da personified an imposing, larger-than-life religious figure. It was difficult to reconcile that presence with an image of him swinging a golf club. I sometimes wonder why he never told us of these outings. Certainly, it was not *de rigueur* for a reverend minister to *shlep* his golf bag over the links in Wicklow, or elsewhere, for that matter.

Our summer holidays in Wicklow provided me with the happiest memories of my youth. With no secular or Hebrew school to attend during July and August, summers were free and fun. Amy tagged along, so my parents could enjoy their holidays as well. She was a sweet girl with a gentle manner, and we loved her and considered her part of the family.

We stayed in a cottage by the sea. I can hear, still, the clatter of the milkman's horse and buggy, as he delivered fresh milk from the dairy. At the first sounds of the buggy in the distance, I would race out of the house to meet him.

"What've we here?" he'd say, greeting me with a wave. "And how are you this morning, young master?"

"Fine, sir," I'd say, squinting up at him. The morning sun always rose just above his shoulder.

After he placed the bottles of milk on our stoop, he'd look at me and wink. "I'm a bit short-handed today. Do you know of anyone who might come along for the ride?"

He always smiled at my enthusiasm. I loved that buggy! It wasn't a simple contraption like you'd see on a farm, but a more elegant type that might be used for a Sunday outing. The bench was cushiony, and in the rear stood tall pewter cans full of milk and a long, metal ladle that wavered in the breeze.

"Well, go and ask your mammy and daddy if it'd be all right for you to come along and help me."

I rushed back into the house and, gasping for breath, repeated the milkman's invitation. "Can I, Ma?"

She looked at me with hesitance. "I don't know."

"Please!"

She then smiled and relented, "All right, but don't work too hard, and put on a sweater."

A minute later, I was climbing up and taking my place alongside the milkman. As the buggy made its way along the streets of Wicklow, the ladle knocked and clanged, alerting families to ready their empty bottles. It was so many years ago, but I'll never forget bouncing up and down the country roads and narrow lanes, servicing homes throughout the town.

The beach was filled with pebbles of all shapes and sizes, beautiful stones, polished smooth from years of waves washing over them. They were a myriad of colors, and when the morning sun struck the beach, they glistened in a rainbow of hues. We would pile these stones and then try to knock them down by throwing a larger stone at them. These target games were fiercely competitive between my siblings and me, and our friends. We relished our time playing on the sand and bathing in the Irish sea.

Most days we'd settle ourselves at the end of a long pier jutting out into the sea and go fishing, our feet dangling over the water. It was deep right off the pier, and we caught loads of fish: plaice, whiting, and cod. Some, we threw back, and others, we kept and cleaned for dinner.

Adjacent to the pier were a number of large, odd-shaped rocks. We would climb on them and play games. Sometimes, the waves hit just right and sent a huge spray of water over us – how delightful! A small gap between the rocks formed a natural hole, which fed down to the sea. Now and then, we'd drop a line there and fish for crabs and lobsters.

I know what you're thinking: *a Jewish boy fishing for crab and lobster?* Yes, they're treif and forbidden to eat.

"What's this?" my father asked, when we brought him a pail full of crabs.

"Bait!" we declared.

"Very good, children, thank you." Da placed the bucket aside and focused his eyes on the sea.

As any fisherman knows, patience and perseverance are essential skills to have. There are those who spend an entire day at sea, come home with nothing in their pail, and consider the day a success. My father, though quite adept at putting fish in his pail, was one of these men. He could spend a whole day on the pier, casting his line, his eyes fixed on the water. Fishing was a hobby my mother and father enjoyed together. Ma would join him on the pier, and Da would set aside his fishing pole and ready her line for casting. In these moments, I saw the devotion they had for each other.

While on holiday, my father seemed to discard the weight of his position at the synagogue. Perhaps he chose to vacation in a place with fewer Jews so he could unwind. Enjoying the serenity of our holidays, the war receded into the distance. My parents often rowed into the deep, black waters of the Irish Sea. They'd be out all night, fishing under the stars, the waves splashing gently against the boat. Here, Da was no longer the cantor of the shul, but simply a man out with his wife, enjoying nature. A boy of twelve, I had little appreciation for that. What excited me was the warm sun on my back as I ran and played with other children along the pebbled beach.

The Wicklow River was home to summer boat races, serious affairs, in which large sums of money were wagered. Competing towns arrived in Wicklow with their own rowing skiffs and crews, who were gritty boatmen. Citizens of the various towns lined the riverbank, cheering their team. My loudest cheers were for the Byrne brothers, with whom I felt a personal connection, having visited their shop and having watched them build the skiffs. The races were followed by celebrations that lasted well into the night. Those were enchanting times indeed.

Competitive and fun-loving, my siblings and I foot-raced all the time. Our first summer in Wicklow held a particular joy for me as that was the year my leg brace came off. I quickly proved to be an able runner, darting over the rocky beach.

"Look at Theo run!" Ma shouted.

My father smiled with pride. "I knew he'd be fine."

"Did you?"

"Of course. Theo has always been a strong boy."

"I wish I could have been so sure."

The doctors hadn't promised anything about the outcome of my surgeries. Ma posed the question directly, "Will he be able to keep up with the others?"

"Every child is different," they said. "Only time will tell."

The most optimistic forecasts could not have predicted me running along the beach as I did that summer. My recovery was so astonishing to grown-ups that they named me "Samson," after the biblical hero. "Samson, you're even faster than yesterday!" they'd encourage me.

I met their observation with bashful pride, never thinking that I would one day run as fast as my brother and sisters – faster even. I

83

ran like a frisky colt, and it was exhilarating! I will always associate the joys of that new freedom with Wicklow.

In time, I befriended some non-Jewish children. A group of eight or ten of us would go off to a place called the Murrough, not far from the pier. It was an enormous field of grass overlooking the sea, where we played rugby and football or simply enjoyed a picnic lunch. The railroad bordered the field, and we watched trains coming and going. Nearby, a hill shielded us from view, and we'd sit around and talk, and smoke woodbines – cheap cigarettes you bought by the piece. A few years later, we'd go there to neck with the girls. "Spin the Bottle" was a favorite game, and kissing the chosen was always a thrill.

Looking back on these summers, I have come to realize that as children, there wasn't much difference between "us" and "them." We went to synagogue, and they, to church. We didn't discuss religion. We enjoyed each other's company as teenage boys and girls do.

* * *

North of Wicklow, at Sandycove, there is a swimming hole known as "a gentleman's bathing place," called the "Forty Foot" – its name owing, not to its depth, but to the Fortieth Regiment, once stationed in the area. The Forty Foot was the domain of a swimming club reserved for men; many were naturists who swam in the nude. A deep seawater inlet, it attracted swimmers who braved its waters even through the winter months. The surrounding cape sheltered male bathers from the prying eyes of ladies, until the women's liberation movement of the 1970s, when women also began swimming there. Today there is a sign that reads "Togs Must Be Worn." Nearby stands the famous Martello Tower, where James Joyce stayed briefly in

1904. The tower is described in the opening chapter of *Ulysses* and is now the home of the James Joyce Museum.

Of course, the local history did not impress me as a boy, and I never was a swimmer. I was much happier in the calm, shallow waters near the cottage. With my brace off and already twelve, Da thought it was time I learned to swim, and Forty Foot was his choice for teaching me. Today, what we call swimming instruction, my father would have described as coddling, and he would have none of that. His logic was to place a child in the water and, like an animal, they'll swim naturally. This, I was unaware of.

Amy and Abey were looking after the girls at the cottage, when we arrived at Sandycove. I took a little walk, climbed onto the giant rocks near the swimming area, and looked out on Dublin Bay – a picturesque view, with sailboats and a fishing vessel in the distance. It was a cool and cloudy morning. I breathed in deeply the sea air, and, though fearful and reluctant, thought: *today I'm going to make my parents proud and learn to swim in water over my head.*

"Do you think he's ready?" Ma asked nervously.

"Of course, he's ready."

I'm sure she wasn't convinced. Through the years, my infirmity caused my mother to be protective of me, and as the second son, even more so. Jewish tradition is curious on this matter. It's clear from the Bible that the elder son is meant to inherit his father's wealth and blessing, however, in the stories of the Old Testament, it is the younger who does.

My father dismissed her concerns, took me by the hand, and walked me down the cement stairs that led to the sea. I thought he would enter the water first and demonstrate swimming technique, starting with treading water; I heard it was like riding a bicycle, which I was good at. And after getting the hang of it, I would then practice some strokes, keeping close to the steps, in case I needed them.

But I soon found out this was not Da's way. As his father taught him, and likely in generations before, on that summer's day in August 1941, he picked me up and tossed me into the sea, away from the steps. I remember thrashing about in the cold, salty bay, panic stricken! I doubt if I ever got my head above water and was fished out by a young gentleman before I drowned.

"*Kol hakavod!* (well-done), Theo," my father said proudly. "It's a good first lesson." I didn't answer him; I was busy coughing up water from my lungs. . . After, I decided not to say anything.

I ran up the stairs and into Ma's arms, "Never again!" I shouted. Reticent, she held me close; but it was all I needed. "Let's go home," I said, fed up with the whole experience. Surely, I despised my father for a time.

A few years would pass before I learned to swim as a young teen at a Jewish summer camp. Esther Baker, who was a good friend and a great swimmer, taught me.

"I'll never swim."

"Yes, you will!"

I shook my head. "When it comes to me and water, I'm dead weight."

She laughed. "I'll teach you."

There was a good deal in her manner that made her teaching preferable to my father's.

"And you know the best part?" she said.

"What?"

"You won't have to do anything."

"How's that?"

"All you have to do is relax and float." Of course, I didn't believe her. But sure enough, she positioned me on my back, let go, and I floated. In time, I was able to do some strokes, and before long, I was swimming at the Forty Foot!!

Chapter 12
Father Seamus

In Wicklow, aside from our circle of friends, we had contact with prominent non-Jews, including the mayor and one of the town's venerable priests. Occasionally, on a Sunday, we'd be invited as a family to the homes of local citizens for tea. Our Jewishness was treated with a mixture of politeness and curiosity. While we children played in their beautiful gardens, eating blackberries and raspberries off the vine, our parents would engage in conversation. My father's views were sought after on several topics, including politics, the Jewish crisis in Europe, and religion in general.

Da was insightful and a powerful presence, who won their admiration. But he was careful to hold these relationships at arm's length. His caution was instinctual; he was polite to non-Jews and always remembered his place in a gentile world.

Because our lives were immersed in Jewish ways, I was fascinated to observe how he and my mother behaved in the presence of Gentiles. Not only did we visit their homes, but my parents received them in ours. In Wicklow, a visit from a non-Jew of standing thrust our home into a beehive of activity – this was seen as a major event. After all, we were representing Jewish family life. I volunteered to polish the silver on these occasions, as my parents naturally wanted to display our best finery.

"Hurry, they'll be here soon!" Ma would say, as we made our home pristine. When guests arrived, there were warm greetings and introductions. After dinner, the men proceeded to the study to have a brandy, light a cigar, and talk, while the women shared tea in the parlor. If a male guest came alone, Ma would sit with her embroidery.

Although the company of a priest made me a bit nervous, I enjoyed Father Seamus' visits to our home. He was an astute fellow with a quick wit and lively eyes that took in everything at once. My father braced for these encounters as he would for battle, girding himself for an intellectual and spiritual discourse. Each time they met, Father Seamus, true to the directive of the Catholic Church, would try valiantly to save Da's soul, as though his priestly mission on Earth would be complete if he succeeded. His efforts were a delightful exercise in futility.

"But surely, your reading of Genesis demonstrates the doctrine of sin," Father Seamus began, as he always did, with the fall of man as recorded in the Garden of Eden.

"That we sin is not the same concept as original sin, as articulated by the Church," Da said in reply.

Their discussion would take a familiar path and then hit upon something new and unexpected. Father Seamus might refer to Isaiah's prophecies of the Virgin Birth.

"In Hebrew, those prophecies only speak of 'maiden' or 'young girl,'" my father said, his expertise with the Hebrew language clarifying the text.

"But surely, a maiden is understood to be a virgin," the priest said, attempting to bolster his argument for the Immaculate Conception. They talked about the meaning of "messiah" and the concepts of grace and forgiveness, while exploring the nuances of the Kol Nidre prayer recited on Yom Kippur eve.

Ultimately, they discussed Jesus and his life. My father was aware of the Church's mostly anti-Jewish history and slanderous preaching of the Blood Libel – an absurd and unfounded accusation that Jews baked Passover matzas with the blood of sacrificed Christian children. He knew of the zeal of Church missionaries who, centuries before, had driven the Jews of Spain and Portugal into hiding, to save their lives and preserve their religion.

Da was under no illusion as to how far he could go in arguing the identity of Jesus, even with a kind soul like Father Seamus. He would broach the subject with gentle humor. "Father Seamus, you must remember that Jesus was born a Jew, lived as a Jew, and his teachings were Jewish teachings."

"Now, that's not entirely true –"

"Father Seamus, his visit to the Temple when he turned over the tables of the money changers was most likely his Bar Mitzvah, when he was called to manhood as a Jew. The Last Supper was, undoubtedly, a Passover seder. Jesus lived and died a Jew." After a dramatic pause, he added, "And so shall I."

* * *

As I think back, these discussions were tragically underscored a short time later, when news reached us that the Warsaw Ghetto had been established the previous November. To give you an idea of what misery it was to be imprisoned in this ghetto:

> 460,000 Jews lived in an area encompassing 1.3 square miles, with an average of nine people per room, subsisting on meager food rations. By the time the Nazis had demolished the ghetto in

May of 1943, at least 300,000 Jews were killed by bullet or gas, and an additional 92,000 died of starvation and disease. (Wikipedia)

"What has the world come to?" my mother asked in horror, knowing only too well.

Our hopes were lost that day, with our relatives' fate sealed in that vile ghetto. A year later, in a two-month span, from July 22nd to September 21st of 1942, nearly all of 300,000 surviving Jews – among them, nearly two hundred members of our family – were delivered to the Treblinka death camp, and, upon arrival there, murdered in the gas chambers.

I have kept and still treasure the family correspondence we received throughout the 1930s and into early 1940, including a handful of letters my parents mailed to Poland and Belgium – letters that never reached their destination but were returned to our home stamped "opened by censor." The censor, of course, was a Nazi agent.

Henri ROSENSTRAUCH
78, Rue du Pélican, ANVERS

OPENED BY CENSOR — P.C. 66

AN SCRÚDÚDÓIR D'OSCAIL — OPENED BY CENSOR

PER VLIEGTUIG

Rev. W. Jarbarz
73, S.C. Rd. Portobello
Dublin
Eire / Ireland

Postcard from Wolf to Harry dated June, 1940 Stamped "No Service, Return to Sender"

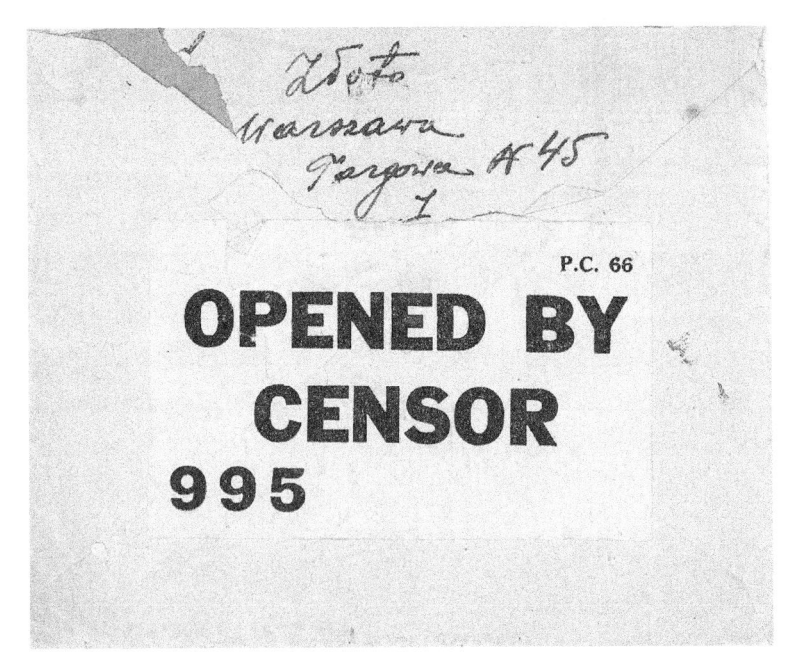

War-time letter to Wolf & Rachel from family residing at 45 Targowa, Warsaw, Poland

Other than we who lived in Ireland, the only survivors in our extended family were a cousin, Beryl Garbarz, who boarded the steamship Austria in 1940, en route to Buenos Aires, a younger cousin, Tadeusz, who was ferried off to Switzerland, and an aunt, *Ciotka* Eugenia, with her daughter and grandson, who remained in Poland. They had wealth and survived with the help of Polish Catholics living in Warsaw.

The Jewish press in various countries received word of the Nazi atrocities in code – secret messages that spread globally and became the subtext of our daily lives. The mainstream press in Ireland, England, and the United States, however, remained silent. Whispered gossip moved among families like fire on dry tinder, but we were helpless to intervene.

All we could do was to send food, money, and clothing to our loved ones in Poland during the 1930s, through committees that were organized when Hitler first began his march to power. Millions of European Jews were suffering unbearable poverty. Rev. Wolf Garb was instrumental in raising monies for the United Kingdom's branch of charities that came to their aid. These included the World Mizrachi Organization of Great Britain and Ireland; the Jewish National Fund Commission for Dublin; the Dublin Committee for Relief of Jews in Eastern Europe; the Joint Passover Relief Appeal; and the Chief Rabbi's Religious Emergency Fund for German and Austrian Jewry.

Rev. Wolf Garb, Dublin (1930s)

Da also served as the visiting minister to hospitals, nursing homes, and prisons. Occasionally, Jewish prisoners would be housed in Dublin's Mountjoy Gaol prison. During the war, some were arrested for their involvement in the black-market trading of ration coupons. The prison authorities knew of my father's singing talents and invited him to organize their Christmas concert.

How frightened I was the first time I accompanied him through the black steel gates of Mountjoy Prison on a Christmas Eve. Prison guards and Irish police (*Garda Siochana*) were milling around, keeping order. I can still hear the chilling clang of the metal doors as we passed inside. The mess hall was turned into a theatre, a small wooden stage and wooden chairs set in place. I remember sitting in the front row next to the governor of the prison and his wife. Despite the bleak *environs*, the concert was a smashing success, with its broad involvement of the inmates, both as performers and as an audience for my father's impassioned singing of operatic arias and Irish song.

Judaism has a strong directive to take care of those in difficult circumstances and those less fortunate. An entire chapter in Leviticus, referred to as the "Holiness Code," outlines how we are to care for the poor. In Ireland, there were many poor Jews, but thanks to the Jewish Board of Guardians, none of them wanted for clothing, food, or shelter. Many children of these families went on to university and rose to prominence in their fields of endeavor.

Ireland, though a tolerant country, did not allow carte blanche immigration; it was selective. Relatives had to sponsor immigrants, proving they had the financial means to support these new arrivals, until they became self-reliant. It was no different anywhere else, including the United States, where immigration quotas also applied. Who would take in the Jewish refugees of Eastern and Central Europe?

We listened, spellbound, to Hitler's tirades on European radio as did his millions of willing followers. Although he spoke in German, I could understand bits and pieces of what he said, thanks to my growing knowledge of Yiddish, in part derived from German. As the news grew dire, my parents still hoped for the well-being of our relatives. Ma would sit with her embroidery, her face distant, perhaps thinking of her family in Poland and Belgium, and of her youth, remembering how life was good. Could generations of Jewish families be wiped off the face of the earth? And for what? For being Jewish?

It was unfathomable, and yet, real. As real as Father Seamus' visits to our summer home. Nothing could shake my father's devotion to Judaism at any time, and when Jews were being slaughtered and our communities destroyed, he remained steadfast in his resolve to ease his people's suffering. God had determined who my father would become, but my own identity and future had yet to be revealed.

. .

Chapter 13

A Boy Becomes a Man

Growing up, I attended synagogue every Shabbos and every Jewish holiday – now that's a lot of shul! As an infant and toddler, I sat with my mother in the balcony, the women's section, absorbing the sounds of Hebrew prayer. At seven years of age, my formal religious training began. I attended cheder with other children, and together, we learned the *aleph-beis,* the Hebrew alphabet. This developed into reading and writing Hebrew, discussing bible stories, and, over the years, the study of Jewish culture, Jewish history, and observance.

Our teachers, strict and demanding as they were, continued a warm and lovely tradition established by the ancient rabbis. On our first day of Hebrew School, they placed a small candy on the second page of our textbook. We were all excited to learn the first page, so we could turn it and enjoy the sweet reward. In this way, our teachers affirmed that learning is sweet.

Learning the aleph-beis was a practical matter, a means to a specific end. We didn't learn Hebrew in the sense that we could speak or even read it with understanding. We learned to decode the letters, so we could pick up a *siddur* (prayer book) and pray. Our chanting of the Hebrew liturgy involved a more intuitive than literal understanding. As we immersed ourselves in the music and rhythms of the ancient texts, we derived a spiritual connection to our ancestors and a closeness with God.

At twelve, in addition to cheder, I began private studies with Rabbi Brown. He was the kind of teacher familiar to many Jews, reminding me of the colorful characters found in the Sholem Aleichem stories. Many times, the character who seems, at first, to be the least appealing – a beggar or teacher in rags – turns out to be the Messiah in disguise (a Messiah who assesses the virtue of the Jewish community by how he is treated while veiled as a pauper). These stories made me look at Rabbi Brown and wonder: *could he be the Messiah?*

There were a number of "Rabbi Browns" in the Dublin community. I became familiar with them, not as characters from a Sholem Aleichem story, but from a darker, sadder tale. They were Holocaust survivors cut adrift from their families and communities in Europe, wandering Jews who carried with them visions of worlds destroyed in a moment.

Rabbi Brown arrived in Dublin without family as a young refugee from Lithuania. The Jewish Board of Guardians helped him secure a modest room to live in. He would visit our homes and teach us Torah for pennies a session. My parents treated Rabbi Brown with respect and hospitality, but I could see pity in Ma's expression when he came to our door.

Short and wizened, he presented a sad figure, tottering along the cobbled streets of Dolphin's Barn, hunched over a walking stick, tapping his way. He was an eccentric sort of fellow who had his *mishegas* (craziness), as he wore several layers of clothing all the time. When he visited our house, he often had on two shirts, two jackets, and two overcoats. He'd walk in, greet us, and proceed immediately to the lesson, without shedding even one of those layers. As we began to study, he would peel off a layer or two.

"*Siz mir heis,*" he'd say in Yiddish, meaning that he was very hot.

A smile would curse my lips. Of course he was hot; he was wearing clothing for two people! But moments later, he would announce that he was cold and put them back on again.

It was hysterical to me but, not wishing to embarrass him, I stifled my laughter. Looking back, I realize how very sad his ritual was. He wasn't physically cold or hot. The wartime horrors he witnessed had created both a freezer and a furnace in his soul, reflected in the layers of clothing he alternately piled on and removed. This ritual continued throughout the lesson and ended only during a meal. Naturally, my mother always insisted that he stay and eat with us.

"So, how is Theo doing with his studies, Rabbi?" my father would ask respectfully.

Rabbi Brown would glance up from his soup and bread, and say humbly, "Baruch Hashem." This was his way of conveying that I was progressing nicely. Under his tutelage, I studied the ancient Torah commentaries and culled from the wisdom of Rashi and Maimonides, among other scholars of note. One text that I found interesting was the *Shulchan Aruch* – the "Prepared Table" – a book that defines the laws of Jewish living. I was thus guided in how life as an observant Jew could be lived in both a meaningful and enjoyable way.

Rabbi Brown, Dublin, Ireland (1942)

To further prepare for my Bar Mitzvah, I studied eight months with Mr. Lev, the headmaster at Zion Schools. My task was to learn the Torah reading and *haftorah* (selection from the prophets) of that Shabbos, along with their blessings. Eventually, I was confronted with the unparalleled event in a Jewish boy's life – my Bar Mitzvah.

The Bar Mitzvah is the traditional ceremony that confirms a boy has become a "man" – one who now takes on greater responsibility in his home, synagogue, and community. But what does it mean to become a man while the whole of European Jewry is being threatened with destruction? Wounded souls would gather around our dining table, their grim, stunned expressions often focused on me. What was a young lad to make of all this? Where was my place in this troubled and tenuous world?

My parents did all they could to ensure that we children lived normal and happy lives. On occasion, we entertained guests who came for dinner. The grown-ups would retire to the parlor for a cup of tea, and my siblings and I would then be called in to perform.

"Let's have some music!" my father would announce.

Abey, myself, and our sisters, Lucy and Sarah, had inherited lovely voices. The girls also played piano. Together, we formed a small "Von Trapp" style family. My brother would lead as we performed a broad range of music, from cantorial and operatic pieces to Yiddish and Irish folk songs.

I played the violin now for a few years and was reasonably adept with the instrument. Sarah and I did duets, occasionally joined by my good friend, Bevan Stein, a budding violinist. At the time, Bevan's family, the Cleins, owned the famous Bretzel Bakery & Café in Dublin. Sarah and Bevan would eventually perform their own duet in marriage, the year, 1952; Sarah was but seventeen. Despite her tender age, both sets of parents approved the match.

After our impromptu recitals, my parents and their guests would heartily applaud as we took our bows. Ma was effusive in her praise, shouting, "What voices! What talent!" We were all grateful to be transported away from our fear and sadness. Music was more than a simple distraction; it was our salvation.

"A person who can sing is a person who can live," my father said more than once.

Then Da took center stage, not as a singer, but as a comedian. His jokes were in Yiddish and somewhat off-color. With timing reminiscent of the great Borscht Belt comics, he would stand before his guests and deliver one of his favorite jokes. "What's the difference between a *tuchas* and an orange?" He would pause, one second, two, three... until the very silence cried out for the answer. "Give a *shmek, ves du vissen!*" (Smell them and you'll know!)

I loved to hear my father tell such jokes, jokes that young men might whisper to one another both for laughs and for a sense of being alive. Life can be a gritty affair, and when you've been persecuted like the Jews or the Irish, well, you work through the pain with laughter. With my Bar Mitzvah fast approaching, I took every opportunity to laugh.

The event was daunting enough for any boy, but my Bar Mitzvah, as a cantor's son and a shy lad, was a momentous affair. The expectations people had of me to chant fluently and beautifully, at times, were overwhelming. Five hundred people would attend services that day, expecting a stellar rendition. But the eyes that I would feel most acutely were my father's. He would be measured this day as well.

"Everything comes down to thirty minutes," I said glumly to my brother.

Abe laughed and slapped me on the shoulder. "C'mon, we've all been through it. You'll live."

I took little solace in his words.

Theodore Garb on the eve of his Bar Mitzvah (1942)

Finally, the Sabbath morning of July 11, 1942, arrived. Seated next to the rabbi and facing the congregation, I looked out at a sea of men, their *talleisim* (prayer shawls) draped over their heads and shoulders. Lifting my eyes to the balcony, I exchanged glances with my mother and sisters, who nodded and smiled their support for me.

As the service began, I barely heard the prayers; I was numb, awaiting the awesome moment of truth when I would be called to the Torah as a Bar Mitzvah. An hour and a half later, my father announced in melody to all:

"*Ya'amod habachur habarmitzvah, Tuvia ben Reb. Zev veRachel...*" (The Bar Mitzvah boy will rise, Theodore, son of Rev. Wolf and Rachel.)

I stood and walked to the *bimah*, my legs dragging like lead weights. I could feel the shul's attention focus on me. My father's eyes smiled with pride as I steadied myself with a white-knuckled grip, holding fast to the table where the Torah lay. Slowly, I wrapped the *tzitzis* (tallis fringe) around my index finger and touched it to the holy Torah parchment, then kissed the fringe and proceeded to chant the Torah blessing as strongly as I could. "*Bar'chu es Adonai ham'vorach...*"

Five hundred souls responded in unison, "*Baruch Adonai ham'vorach l'olam va-ed.*" After I sang half the blessing, my father handed me the sterling silver *yad* (pointer) and, in a moment, I was chanting from the Torah with all my heart (*parashas* – the portion of – *Matos Masei*), and completed the reading without a mistake. Phew! I then finished chanting the blessing.

Next came the haftorah and its blessings, an easier challenge (with vowels included in the text), though a much lengthier reading. Well-prepared, as I chanted the haftorah, I felt liberated, free to express my love for singing Hebrew liturgy (which carried into my adult life, and which I shared with my children).

Afterward, the congregation wished me "*Simmen Tov and Mazel Tov,*" a song of congratulations and blessing. Looking up to my mother, I could see her eyes tearful with joy. My father, beaming, judged well by his congregation, then recited the traditional prayer for the parent of a Bar Mitzvah. In it, he thanked God for releasing him of responsibility for my actions – now, I was to be held accountable for my behavior.

Standing frozen before the ark, my heart pounding as he chanted this blessing, the rise and fall of his voice created a mood of profound solemnity. At the conclusion of services, I was escorted from pew to pew so that everyone could give me their warm wishes and a hearty mazel tov, then ushered to the balcony, where the women pinched and patted my cheeks and told me what a lovely job I had done. With the fullness of their attention on me, I fairly blushed.

As a Bar Mitzvah, I would now be discussed in mature terms. In most Orthodox families, young men and women were expected to marry at eighteen (and surely by twenty), in accordance with Jewish law. Often, these marriages were arranged to fulfill that expectation.

Fortunately, just as my mother had refused to wear a sheitel, there were certain areas where my parents deviated from tradition. This was one of them, as they were never inclined to arrange unions for their children. But they did expect us to observe Jewish laws governing proper behavior between the sexes.

As in most aspects of life, the Orthodox way of courting was quite rigid. What our parents didn't teach us about sex, we learned from each other. Having earned a reputation as something of a teenage Casanova, my brother would later be a wealth of knowledge for me. And so, having formally passed into Jewish adulthood, I was on the threshold of adult society, with adventure on the horizon and many lessons yet to be learned.

Chapter 14
War's End: Picking Up the Pieces

Over the next few years, as the war raged on, we lived the best we could. As my mother would say, "Life is for the living." Young people fell in love and were married. There continued to be births and brises. We celebrated these blessings in our lives just as we had during peacetime. *L'chayim!* (to life) we cried, the toast of the Jewish people.

The rabbis delivered a similar message from the pulpit: "We must not let the world's violent convulsions spoil our expressions of joy and thanksgiving." This determination existed even in the very depths of hell – the concentration camps – where Jews and others were being crushed by Hitler's enmity. The time-honored rituals of our people were celebrated, still: the Sabbath was observed with bits of wax and saved bread, and Passover seders were concluded with the same ringing hope proclaimed in Jewish homes around the world – *next year in Jerusalem!*

Was it blindness or fantasy that fueled this resolve to see the beauty of life amid the ashes of the camps? No, it was faith – faith in the one God of Israel and humanity. We survived. We lived!

My passage into manhood was one of two watershed events in my youth. The other came with the end of the war, a bittersweet victory for the Jewish people. Finally, the nightmare was over, and we who survived looked forward to helping rebuild the shattered lives of our brethren. Tears of joy and relief filled our home on May 8, 1945.

"God has answered our prayers," my father sighed.

Almost immediately, he and my mother began to investigate what had become of our family in Poland and Belgium. Would my parents venture to Poland, where more than two hundred of our relatives had lived before the war? There were rumors of Polish attacks on Jews returning home to search for loved ones and to reclaim their properties; those were trying days.

How to reach the continent while hordes of refugees were leaving – that was the question. There was terrible confusion as The Red Cross and Jewish agencies were assisting thousands upon thousands of displaced persons, survivors of what would ultimately be known as the *Shoah,* the Holocaust.

My parents chose not to go to Poland; instead, they went to Belgium. Five years had passed without a word from Ma's family. All through it, she was strong for us, but the strain was evident.

"What's taking so long?" she asked my father.

"There is a great deal of paperwork to do."

"I don't care about paperwork!"

Da used his influence to gain passage and my parents left for Antwerp in search of Grandpa Solomon, Grandma Taube, and Uncle Harry. Before the war, my maternal grandfather was a multi-millionaire. There was property, cash, diamonds, and artwork to recover. But had anyone or anything survived?

Da later described arriving in Antwerp, where he and Ma discovered a Europe worse than they could have imagined. Civilization had been reduced to rubble; destruction was everywhere. "The physical destruction was one thing," my father said, his voice thick with emotion, "but what happened to the people. . ."

Antwerp was teeming with those desperate to eat, to find shelter, and to locate missing parents, wives, husbands, sons, and daughters. Tens of thousands who once lived whole and joyous lives were as walking shadows on the streets of Antwerp.

They walked along, lost in once familiar streets; the rubble and their emotions conspired to disorient them. After several wrong turns, they came to the apartment building on the Pelikanstrasse (78 Rue du Pelican), where my mother's family had lived. The complex was still intact. My father knocked on the apartment door.

"Who's there?" a neighbor asked, peering into the hallway. "What do you want?"

"Our relatives lived here," my father answered in Flemish. "Do you know where they are?"

The neighbor shrugged, "No."

"When did you last see them?"

The man thought for a moment and said, "It's been years. They've not been here for years."

At that point, my mother's heart sank.

"I will help you," the man said. He ducked into his apartment and returned with a small crowbar. As they worked to pry open the apartment door, the man offered that he had been somewhat friendly with Ma's family.

"Of course, they were more frightened than we were," noting that he and his family were not Jewish. "We didn't think such things could ever happen here."

My father had an instinctive suspicion of anyone claiming ignorance or innocence. Still, he was grateful for the assistance.

The door opened, and Wolf and Rachel took their first cautious steps inside. The first thing that struck them was the smell, a musty stench like the inside of a crypt. The curtains hung limp against the windows; dim sunlight filtered in. Slowly, stoically, they walked further inside. The apartment was mostly unchanged from several years earlier, tastefully furnished and pleasing to the eye. They stepped into the dining room and gazed in horror – before them, a cruel moment frozen in time. . . The table was set for the Sabbath: fine china, crystal wine glasses, and silver lay on embroidered cloth. A whole roasted chicken, now bones, and a challah, now petrified and moldy, waited to be served. Unlit Shabbos candles stood tall, witness to the Friday night when the Gestapo came and took Grandpa Solomon and Grandma Taube away, as they sat down to their Shabbat dinner.

"They desecrated the Shabbos," my father said, his voice filled with rancor. "They shamed the name of God."

There is no record of what became of my grandparents; we assume they met their fate in the concentration camps, along with Ma's two sisters, Miriam and Hinda, their husbands and children, who lived in Poland. As for Ma's brother, my Uncle Harry, well, Abey shared with me this in later years:

> Our Uncle Harry, as I recall, was personal diamond broker and friend to King Alfonso of Spain. In his heyday, Harry was a dashing, young man-about-town, elegant, and dressed to the nines. When female celebrities visited Belgium, he would take them in tow and be their escort to restaurants and places of entertainment. In one photograph, I remember him with Greta

Garbo. I recall a report stating that when the Gestapo came looking for him, they tortured his girlfriend to reveal where he was hiding, and eventually, he was shot crossing the border into France with a million British pounds worth of diamonds in his possession.

Any remaining family wealth was also confiscated by the Nazis. Ma never spoke of her return to Antwerp; her grief was overwhelming. Da, however, shared their grim experience one evening. He then opened a letter he wrote to Zeyde in 1940 that was returned, citing "no service, return to sender."

As my father showed us the letter, he said, "Here, I used to write. More than once, I begged Zeyde to come to Ireland, to bring his family and fortune here to our Garden of Eden. And do you know what he would say? 'Life is good in Belgium, *our* Garden of Eden.'" Da's voice trailed off to a whisper, "He didn't know the serpent would enter that garden."

For Jews, the allied victory put an end to the ordeal, but oh, so many lives were lost. The world of European Jewry was shattered. Even for those who were not eyewitness to these events, it would be a long time before horrific images did not shadow our thoughts and our days. . .

Uncle Harry & Grandpa Solomon, Antwerp, Belgium (1920s)

Chapter 15
Teen Social Groups

While we lived in a society where Jews and non-Jews mixed, our early social lives were dominated by Jewish social and cultural groups. Prominent among these was *Habonim* (the Builders), a Jewish version of America's Boy Scouts and Girl Scouts, for children twelve to sixteen years of age.

Founded in London, in the late 1920s, Habonim attracted a large following. By the time a leadership handbook was published shortly after its first year, several groups had been organized throughout England. Habonim quickly became an official movement under the auspices of the British Zionist Federation. Like the Boy Scouts and Girl Scouts, there was a clear structure and curriculum. As a Zionist youth movement, Habonim activities were devoted to "The Holy Land," as Israel was known prior to 1948.

We learned Hebrew, Jewish history, and geography. Also, there were outdoor activities, such as camping and athletic events, the importance of which became evident as we prepared for a pioneering role in the early *kibbutzim* (communal farms) of *Eretz Yisro'el,* the land of Israel.

I loved Habonim. It was there that I got my start as something of a public performer. We were taught modern Hebrew songs, and we wrote and acted in plays about a future Israel. One role I played was as a rugged pioneer who transformed the desert into a green place, as the Bible taught, a land flowing with milk and honey.

Along with our regular *tzedakah* box for local charity donations, a second box was for sending money to the Holy Land, to help it become a Jewish homeland once again. Though determined to avoid political or religious agendas, Habonim was certainly influenced by the pioneer movement, which had a socialist bent.

Hanoar was another Jewish club that influenced me, attended mostly by non-Orthodox boys and girls. That meant socializing with those who did not observe as strictly as did the Jewish families in my community. I'll never forget my first time on a picnic outing with Hanoar. I was enjoying the company of new friends when one of the boys put a slice of cheese on his meat sandwich – strictly forbidden in a kosher household, where the mixing of dairy products with meat is not allowed. I couldn't believe it! I was shocked that a Jewish boy would do such a thing. Looking back, who was I to judge? In time, I'd be doing the same.

* * *

In July 1945, I turned sixteen and, later that summer, spent several weeks at Magill's Farm, about twenty miles south of Belfast, near the villages of Donaghadee and Millisle. Ten thousand German, Austrian, and Czech refugee children, ages three to sixteen, were allowed entry into the UK without a visa, some of whom came to the farm. The reason for my being there was twofold: one, to be out of the way of my parents in that immediate post-war period, and two, to do a mitzvah in helping out. Children whose parents were missing or had been killed in the Holocaust lived there until relatives were located or foster homes could be arranged for them. Founded in 1939, this relief effort was co-sponsored by the Belfast and Dublin Jewish communities, as well as the Joint Christian Churches of Ireland.

Magill's was a hundred acres and provided a majestic view of the sea. We swam, fished, played football, and attended Shabbos services in the small prayer room on the farm. For me, the experience was akin to a working holiday: milking cows, harvesting crops, and raking and weeding pastures. Meals were served in a central dining room, and we gathered there to socialize as well. Aunt Jean worked as a cook in the kitchen, and it was wonderful to have family there, a taste of home. Boys and girls worked together on their chores, giving us a chance to mingle throughout the day. During late-night gatherings, we lads would share our fantasies about the opposite sex, though I didn't expect my stay on the farm to change my virgin status.

One evening, while leaving the dining room, I found myself walking with Hannah, a darling girl with whom I was flirting. A moment later, our hands briefly touched. As we continued along, I boldly grasped her hand, wrapping her fingers in mine. She smiled at my advance. For a few minutes, we walked in the moonlight, holding hands and being playful with each other, until we parted with a kiss.

Although I indulged in such flirtations, my experiences on the farm convinced me that I would not be making love with a Jewish girl before marriage. That was tradition! For Jewish boys, sexual initiation was sought with gentile women. We knew the peril of having deep feelings for them – falling in love with a non-Jew could only bring emotional trauma to the couple and their families. Both sides knew that a mixed marriage was to be avoided at all costs.

The Jewish and Irish Catholic communities worried about their sons and daughters becoming romantically involved. While there were a handful of such marriages, they were considered scandalous and brought shame to the respective families. For Catholics, I imagine that marrying within the religion was more a cultural imperative, but for Jews, it was deemed a matter of survival. After all, we were at the end of a war in which the Jews were marked for extinction. For this reason alone, it was incumbent on me to marry a Jewish girl to ensure the continuity of our people.

At the time, I was under the spell of raging hormones, and the forces of Orthodox Judaism began to wane inside me. Before my generation, parents would not have allowed their children to interact with those from non-observant families. But I had ever-increasing contact with less religious boys and girls, and with Gentiles as well, because of my attendance at a secular high school.

Jewish law was firm in matters of sexuality. The laws of tz'niut were clear about how girls and boys were to behave. Orthodox Jewish couples were not allowed to show affection in public. I never saw the parents of my friends hold hands, let alone kiss. Was I ever privy to a moment of affection shown by adults in my youth? – only with my parents, who were in love for so many years.

* * *

If Orthodox Judaism was inflexible when it came to sexual expression, the attitudes of the Catholic Church were carved in stone. Not only were Catholic mores stricter than Jewish sensibilities, as they elevated celibacy to an exalted status, there were issues of political power. By virtue of its dominant political and societal position, the Catholic Church exerted every effort to impose its divine will on the citizens of Ireland.

Censorship was a means to this end. Ireland's censorship laws were more severe than even the most ardent Catholics could fathom. While there were occasional fissures in this blanket censorship, rarely did the kind of explosive sentiment erupt as when *Damaged Goods,* a controversial French play by Eugene Brieux, slipped through the censors and ran for a short time in Dublin. The play made references to venereal disease and, so by definition, addressed illicit sexual relations. After it opened, some in the audience rioted to close the play, while others protested to keep it open. Like many, I attended on the sly to see what all the commotion was about. The play's content wasn't revolutionary, but I think the uproar came about because it called attention to a problem in Irish life.

As a Dublin teen, I became adept at reading between the lines and learned where forbidden things lay. In an environment where complete modesty was expected, a small breach could ignite a young man's fantasies: a glimpse of cleavage, a shapely leg, a bare neck. Books and magazines taught me of worlds that existed behind drawn curtains and locked doors. I knew my first sexual experience awaited me – I had only to come upon it.

Theo Garb (1945)

Chapter 16
Flirtation Gone Awry

High school for me was at Wesley College, a typical English-style Protestant school, distinguished by the prominence of its most famous alumnus, George Bernard Shaw. I was a B+ student, bright enough to excel, but not overly studious. It never occurred to me not to do well in school. The importance of learning and knowledge was stressed throughout my growing years. Jews are not called the "People of the Book" for nothing, and, of course, Ireland possessed a rich literary tradition. But to my youthful mind, the best thing about Wesley College was its coed population, with enough pretty girls to distract me.

Students who misbehaved in class received six strokes of the cane; the headmaster seemed to take pleasure in administering that punishment. Students who had not experienced caning firsthand were informed by those who had, as a boy in the class above mine said, "He makes you pull down your trousers so's you feel it against your bare bum."

"Have you been caned?" I asked him.

He nodded.

"What did you do?"

"I talked out of turn."

My jaw dropped. "Just for that?"

This information was enough to keep me on my toes. I had no desire to invite the cane across my bare bottom, but one day, I found myself summoned to the headmaster's inner sanctum; I knew I was in for it!

The day started uneventfully. I suffered through a literature and math class, and before lunch, there was chemistry and then lab. I enjoyed going to the lab, a large schoolroom filled with beakers and test tubes. My friends and I would pretend we were mad scientists or budding Albert Einsteins. After all, Einstein had won every Jewish boy's respect, though the implications of the new atomic age, both wonderous and frightening, were beyond us.

That day in the lab might have turned out differently had Mary not been present. She was a cute blonde I had known awhile, but lately had become infatuated with her. Naturally, I wanted to show off. We were studying what our teacher called the "explosive reactions" of certain chemicals. Instead of listening to his instructions for the experiment, I was busy trying to get Mary's attention.

"Garb! Are you with me?"

"Yes, sir, sorry," I said, hiding a grin.

He continued to watch me suspiciously. When it came time to mix the chemicals, I did so incorrectly.

"No, Garb!!" the teacher cried out, running over to my workbench.

Too late – the beaker exploded, sending slivers of glass in all directions. Girls screamed. I froze with panic and remorse. It was a miracle that only the teacher was injured, suffering mild skin wounds; it could have been much worse.

"Now you've done it," a friend whispered as our teacher grimaced in pain.

"Well, someone go for the nurse!" he shouted. Within moments, the nurse appeared.

"Lord, it's a wonder no one was killed," she said.

A short time later the dean arrived. "What's happened here?" he demanded. A few fingers pointed in my direction. The dean narrowed his bushy eyebrows. "Come with me, young man."

I looked around for Mary. Her eyes widened with sympathy, and then she looked away. Without speaking, the dean led me to the headmaster's office.

The headmaster, a man who could at times be warm and patient, viewed me severely. "What's this I hear about an explosion in the Chemistry lab?" I lowered my head. "Garb, have you anything to say for yourself?"

"No, sir." *What was there to say?*

"You understand that your misbehavior cannot go unpunished."

I nodded, my eyes to the floor. "I didn't mean to hurt anyone."

"No, of course not. People don't intend outcomes that will get them in trouble," he said, unimpressed with my apology.

"No, sir."

"Can you tell me what you were doing that brought about this calamity?"

"I guess I wasn't paying attention, that's all. Will our teacher be all right?"

"I certainly hope so," the headmaster said, not yielding any ground to me. "I assume that you do as well."

"Oh yes, he's a very nice man." (He was, and I was so sorry for everything.)

"Well, Mr. Garb, if you have such high regard for your teacher, why did you ignore his instructions?"

I couldn't very well say the truth: that I was busy impressing a girl. Instead, I remained silent.

"Please close the door."

"Yes, sir." Walking toward the door, my mind raced with the stories of past canings. My hand trembled as I grabbed the doorknob and pushed the door shut.

"Now, come here," he said. "Drop your trousers and place your hands on the edge of my desk." I did what I was told, without protest, and he raised his cane and commenced with the lashing. I winced with each blow, holding back tears of pain and humiliation.

Later, I shared the story of my caning with friends, embellishing the tale, mind you. The next time we met, Mary smiled so sweetly that it almost made the punishment worthwhile.

I arrived home that day without a word from my father. *Phew! Had the news of the incident remained in school?*

"Theo," he said that evening after dinner, as we sat alone at the table.

"Yes, Da?" He leaned forward, his hands clasped together.

"Have you anything to tell me?" My heart sank. I dreaded his finding me out and had clung to the hope that he was not contacted. I sat back in my chair. "Something at school?"

"Ah yes," I said, lowering my eyes. "There was an accident in the chemistry lab."

"An accident?" he said, restraining his anger.

I looked up misty eyed. "It shouldn't have happened. I just didn't hear the instructions right. I didn't mean for anyone to be hurt."

Da fixed his eyes on me. I could feel him weighing the sincerity of my words. I trembled with fear of the punishment that would be meted out for my transgression.

"It's a terrible thing to hurt someone," he said.

"Yes, it is."

"You will have to apologize to your teacher."

"Of course, I will."

"In writing."

"Okay."

"This is awkward for me."

I knew what he meant. My father was a prominent man in the Jewish community, and our family represented Jewish life to the Irish. My behavior reflected badly on him and our people.

"I'm really sorry, Da."

He was quiet for a moment. "Well, at least that."

Chapter 17

On a Mission in Belfast

...ears, both Abe and I questioned the ...re quietly. Unlike me, a dutiful son, ...tspoken.

..."God wants?" he once asked my father, ... of a religious life. After all, Jewish ...ts, in the Torah, the sacred text spoken

...could accept this truth any longer. The ...es in Jewish youth groups, called many ...e no longer comfortable with orthodoxy ...ts restrictions.

My brother ... ...dical school in the fall of 1946. Our father squashed Abe's dream of becoming an engineer, insisting he become a doctor instead. They quarreled about this, but the decision came down to economics. At the time, medical school was a pittance in Ireland, with tuition and books amounting to fifty quid a year. With such reasonable tuition, my father determined it would be a *shanda* (scandalous) not to attend medical school. And that is why Ireland turned out so many doctors and dentists.

Abe continued to challenge my parents in all manner of behavior. He was not anxious to observe the Sabbath and rarely went to shul. Da was beside himself, not knowing how to deal with him.

Abe was my hero. Strong-willed and independent, he lived above the petty judgments of others. How much influence did he have on me? Some time would pass before I fully came to know. I was a spy in the shadows of rebellion, while Abe was out front, leading the charge. As young men, a foremost symbol of our defiance involved the fairer sex.

* * *

The first time a young man buys a condom is a nerve-racking experience. And when that purchase could end in arrest, well, that ups the ante quite a bit! You see, they could not be legally purchased in Catholic Ireland, so my friends and I traveled to Belfast to get them. In the spring of 1946, during our school holidays, three of us took the train to Belfast, plotting our strategy along the way.

"You do the talking," Shloime said.

"Me?" "Why me?" I asked.

"Because you're the best talker."

I turned to Edwin, who nodded in assent.

"And what will you two do?"

"We'll keep a lookout," Shloime said.

A lookout?

"B-but it's legal in Belfast," I said.

Shloime shook his head, "You're a minor. But even if things go smoothly, bringing them into Ireland is also illegal."

I felt a cold sweat on my brow as I stared down my two compatriots. But they just looked away, and the train rolled on to Belfast...

Now, we'd heard about a certain chemist who was sympathetic to needs such as ours. The boys in Hanoar described him as a kindly old man with white hair. "Talk to him," one of the boys advised us. "He'll treat you right."

Loath to ask directions for fear of giving away our illicit purpose, we got lost on our way to the chemist's shop. We couldn't look strangers in the eye lest they identify us as corrupt youths out to further our immoral behavior. I sensed the mark of Cain upon our foreheads. On the bustling streets of Belfast, with each wrong turn, my panic grew.

"This is crazy," I said. "Let's go into the next chemist we see."

Just then, Edwin pointed with his finger, "There it is." Looking down the street, Shloime and I saw the sign jutting out from the doorway: O'LEARY CHEMIST. "Come on!"

My heart sank. "All right, all right. Give me the money." Shloime and Edwin fished through their pockets and produced a handful of coins. I stuffed them into my trousers and drew a deep breath. "Let's go."

The shop was no more than a hundred meters away, but it seemed like a mile. Everyone we passed reminded me of someone from my childhood. A woman walking with her friend looked like my grammar school teacher. My anxiety intensified as I imagined her waving me over and saying, "Hello, Theo. What a fine young man you've grown into. What are you doing in Belfast?" This was the question that would sink me – what *was* I doing in Belfast!

I kept my head down, but the sudden appearance of a bearded man frightened me even more. What if my father himself were walking on the street? Or perhaps a member of the shul? What would he think, having come to Belfast on some business, if he ran into Chazzan Garb's son? An encounter with such a person would be awkward, and I feared what he might say to Da later on.

"Belfast? You must be mistaken. What would my Theo be doing in Belfast?"

"Oh, it was him all right, with his pal, Shloime, and another boy."

"Belfast?"

Tormented by guilt, but fired-up with desire, I hurried along; the key to satisfying my adolescent dreams lay just ahead.

"Well, here we are," Shloime said.

"Yep, here we are," Edwin chimed in.

I glared at them. "I can see where we are."

"Well, go in," Shloime said.

"I'm going."

"Looks to me like you're just standing there," Edwin teased. "Come on, Theo. People are beginning to stare at us. Oh damn!"

"What's the matter?" I said.

"A copper."

I looked up and, sure enough, an officer was walking toward us.

Panic-stricken, I nearly ran to him and turned myself in. But that moment quickly passed as I realized that we hadn't committed a crime – yet. I gathered courage and, looking at the others, said, "Come with me."

I began to walk boldly toward the policeman, and Shloime and Edwin fell in line. My heart was racing as our paths crossed, but the officer just smiled and greeted us with an "Afternoon, lads."

"Good afternoon, sir," I said, not changing my stride.

"Afternoon," Shloime and Edwin said.

With that, our confrontation with the law had passed. I walked a distance before having the nerve to look back over my shoulder and was relieved to see the officer far down the street, turning a corner.

"That was close," Edwin said.

Shloime and I nodded in agreement.

"What now?" Shloime asked.

I was losing patience. "Let's go," I said, and we turned back toward the chemist – I was not to be denied this time. Shloime and Edwin took their positions outside the shop and watched as I pushed open the heavy glass door. A bell rang out in greeting, and the door closed shut behind me.

The air in the shop felt cool and dry. I wandered through the aisles, gazing at the perfumes and lotions on display. There were medicines, bandages – all sorts of things that caught my attention. Walking through a chemist shop gives one a certain insight into ailments, great and small, as well as thankfulness for not suffering from them.

I made my way to the rear counter. To my chagrin, the chemist I encountered was a young man who was anything but kindly and white-haired. He had a serious demeanor and was direct in his manner. "May I help you?" he asked.

Confused, I glanced over my shoulder. What now? Had we come to the wrong shop? Shloime nodded his encouragement through the glass pane and then disappeared from view. I turned around, and, before I could reply, an elderly woman appeared from the stock room.

"We're short of the toilet water," she said.

The young chemist turned to her. "Try the carton by the delivery door. There should be some left."

"Oh good." She looked up at me and smiled hello before returning to the supply room.

The presence of a woman in the shop was more than I had counted on. My face was flush. What if she would hear me ask for condoms? Or worse – see the chemist hand them to me.

"Well?" he said impatiently.

I looked up and stammered, "I-I. . . umm. . . c-con —"

"What's that? I can't understand you."

I steeled myself and spoke in a whisper. "I'd like to purchase some c-condoms."

He nodded in a knowing fashion. "Prophylactics," he said, his voice not wavering a bit.

My face was on fire. I prayed the woman would not reappear. "Yes, please," I said.

"What size?"

I was bewildered by this question and must have looked it. A quick, not unkind, smile flitted across his lips. "A three-pack? A dozen?"

"Three three-packs, sir."

In a moment, he produced three packages of foil wrapped condoms from a drawer beneath the counter, dropped them into a brown paper bag and said, "That'll be ten shillings, six pence." Without looking up, I counted out the money and placed it before him.

"Thanks then," he said.

"Thank you, sir," I said, taking the bag and hurrying away.

As I pulled open the door, he called after me, "Good luck."

"Well?" Shloime said.

"Let's get out of here." I led the way toward the train station, my legs moving as fast as they could, without breaking into a run.

"Did you get them?" Edwin asked, trying to keep up with me.

"Yes, of course, I got them."

He smiled, "You're amazing, Theo!"

"How many?" Shloime asked.

I stopped and looked at my friends. Grinning, I said, "A three-pack." Then narrowing my eyes, said, "A three-pack for each of us. Do you think you'll be needing more than three?"

Shloime laughed. "I'll be happy if one!"

As we neared the station, I told my cohorts about the young chemist and his female assistant. The anxieties of our quest behind us, we laughed aloud. With rubbers in our possession, nothing could stand in the way of our first sexual experience. There was but one other detail – *where to find a willing partner?*

Chapter 18
Romantic Notions

Soon after, I traveled to Paris for the first time. My stay was brief, but as a student and a tourist, I was enthralled with this magical city: its endless cavalcade of restaurants, theatres, and bookstores. Not only was Paris romantic, it was a place where I could be free of Irish and Jewish laws, and Catholic censorship.

Books like Joyce's *Ulysses* and Frank Harris' *My Lives and Loves* were forbidden in Ireland. To be caught with either was to risk jail and fines. But we all knew of these scandalous books and longed to have them. In fact, I promised to bring back copies for my friends – how to smuggle them in was the question. Customs officials were on the lookout for contraband as well as items for which duty could be charged. There were both legal and moral issues to be considered. By skirting the law, I was putting myself at odds with the stewards of good society.

I recall my nervousness on the day of return. If the books in my suitcase were found, it would not be dismissed as youthful indiscretion. Three copies of *Ulysses* and two of *My Life and Loves* made it clear they were not solely for my delight as a reader, but for distribution – a serious offense. At sixteen, mind you, I didn't fully appreciate the crime I was about to commit or the likelihood of punishment. However, it was not my intention to be caught. I had devised a clever plan for smuggling the books into Ireland.

Upon arriving at port in Eire, I joined the long line of travelers passing through customs. It was a tedious process, helped along by the large number of agents at the gate. I looked over the heads of the people in front of me, scrutinized each of the customs agents and, based on appearances, gauged my chances. I reasoned that the younger agents would be more sympathetic toward a lad hiding forbidden books, but then it occurred to me that they were young enough to think like me and, if that were the case, there'd be no way to fool them.

So, I looked to the older agents who were perhaps doddering enough to let a young man slip through. They might view me as they would their own son or grandson, but that thought raised new concerns for me. Were they strict fathers? Did their son or grandson misbehave? Perhaps they would read the same behavior in me. I finally concluded that one customs agent was as good as another. Meanwhile, I was too far along now to relieve myself of the books – there was no turning back.

"Come along then, lad, come on."

One of the agents, an older man, directed me into his gateway. Clutching my leather suitcase, I stumbled in his direction and halted directly in front of him. I smiled as I handed him my passport and held my breath as he turned its pages. . .

"Paris, eh?" he said, glancing up at me.

"Yes, sir," I said, trying to keep my voice steady.

"I remember as a young lad going to Paris," he said almost wistfully. "A long while ago, I can tell you that."

"Yes, sir," I said, not wishing to be drawn into conversation.

"So, what did you do in Paris?"

I shrugged. "Oh, I visited the Eiffel Tower and a couple of museums."

"That's all?"

"Not much else to do."

"Really? No picture shows? No bookstores?" he smiled.

I could feel the heat creeping up the back of my neck. I had to say something. He'd never believe me if I said I'd not done any of those things. "I. . . I did go to the Folies Bergère," I said sheepishly.

"Yep, I thought so," he said with a chuckle. Changing his tone, he added, "Not that we approve of those things, mind you."

"No, sir," I said. Playing along, I added, "You won't tell my father, will you, sir?"

There was a devilish glint in his eyes. "Worried about your old man finding out, are you?"

I lowered my head. "He's a cantor in a synagogue."

"A what?"

"He sings in a Jewish temple."

"Ah, so you're a Jew?"

"Yes, sir."

"And your father's an important man in the Jewish church?"

I nodded. "He's almost like a priest would be, sir."

I was being drawn deeper into conversation (my own fault!). A bead of sweat formed at my brow, and I casually wiped it off, running fingers upward through my hair.

"And he let you go off to Paris like that?"

"A student trip."

"Well, let's have a look at your suitcase, and then we'll see about what we do or don't have to tell your father, now. How's that?"

My hands struggled with the latches. . . This was the moment of truth – success, or humiliation, fines, and possibly jail. I dared not even blink as he pushed his hands through my clothing. Suddenly, he

137

asked, "What's this, then?" He lifted out my *tallis* (prayer shawl). I reached for it and carefully unwrapped it, revealing five forbidden books. The book covers were titled in Hebrew and English, so they appeared to be Jewish books.

"You use these when you pray?" he asked with curiosity.

"The shawl, yes."

"And the books?"

"One of them. The rest are study books, sir. My father insisted that I take them along with me on holiday."

He took one of the books into his hands, and my heart sank for fear that he would open it and read through some of the pages. In that moment, a man further back in line called out, "Are we going to be here all day, then?"

The agent laid the book down. Instead of responding to the guy, he shook his head, muttering under his breath, "Impatient bloke." Then he grinned, "All right, then, welcome home."

"Yes, sir. Thank you, sir. Good to be back." I quickly wrapped up my books and tallis and hurried away.

Whenever I hear the saying, "Don't judge a book by its cover," I'm reminded of this episode. Looking back on that time in my life, I see how different I was from the boy who stood for hours on a five-pound note, not to violate the Sabbath. Here I was, hiding books that were deemed pornographic, in my tallis! And when my plan worked, I was proud of myself and relieved – certainly not feeling guilty about it.

* * *

Back home, Shloime and Edwin hurried to meet with me.

"So?" they asked anxiously.

I smiled and, handing over the books, said, "My friends, here are your treasures!"

For the next week, we poured through the pages of those books, reading to ourselves and then aloud to each other, returning to favorite passages, pausing only to savor the images conjured up by the words and our vivid imaginations. Having these books was an erotic thrill; our dreams seemed tangible.

A short time later, Shloime, Edwin, and I drove to the Sweet 16 party of a Jewish friend who lived in Cork. We stayed over a few days and, one night, went to a local dance that was attended mostly by Gentiles. We managed to chat up three Catholic girls and, after dancing with them awhile, we left the dance hall together.

One of the girls had the keys to her family's seaside bungalow. Her parents were away, and she invited us to spend the night there. Incredibly, each of us three boys was to have his first sexual experience that evening.

With *My Life and Loves* fresh in mind, now given the chance, I knew exactly what to do. But Meagan was as green as I, and the experience was somewhat anticlimactic. Our desires led us on awkwardly, our passion spent nearly soon as it began.

The next morning, my pals and I were starting back to Dublin, when Shloime turned to me and said, "Well?"

"Well, what?"

"Well, how was it?" he asked, with a playful jab to my ribs.

My emotions were shaken by the encounter, but I was relieved to finally be rid of my virginity. I smiled a glance back at him.

139

"You, too?" I asked.

He nodded, and we both broke into fits of laughter. "Tell me everything!" he said.

"I'm not a cad."

"Oh, shut up with that. Just tell me."

So, bit-by-bit, I did (a retelling surely more wonderful than the affair itself). Having at last crossed the threshold of sex, I felt my masculinity confirmed. For a while, I was cautious around my parents, but they continued to treat me just as they always had. Life was as near perfect as could be, until a letter arrived from Meagan.

I was not expecting her to put her feelings into words; the letter was a wildly romantic expression of teenage love. (I have since learned that losing one's virginity is quite different for a girl than it is for a boy.) This was troubling, but not nearly so much as my father retrieving the mail. Curious as to why a perfumed note in a girl's flowery script was addressed to his younger son, he asked, "Who's Meagan?"

"What?"

Da handed me the opened letter, which spelled out the details of our liaison as well as her feelings toward me.

My father could barely control himself. "Not you, too!" he shouted, referring to Abe's open affairs with different women. Abey challenged Da's patience to no end. I remember being troubled at their shouting matches. At twenty-two, Abe was a grown man with religious and ethical values different from the ones our parents instilled in us. He was a free spirit intent on living his life as he pleased. I watched closely and learned well from him.

Chapter 19

My Zeyde

Every family has its share of unique personalities, each with their own virtues. A special quality was inherent in my Zeyde Shlomo, Wolf's father. If our family were Christian, Zeyde would have been declared a saint. His presence in our household tempered the dominating aura of my father. He personified everything that was good in the world. Where Da was a commanding presence, Zeyde was the whisper of holiness that comforted and soothed us.

They were physically and temperamentally different – hard to believe they were father and son. Da was short, round, loud and domineering. Zeyde was tall, slender, soft-spoken, and meek. Intellect and creativity are the traits they shared.

When Da brought Zeyde to Ireland from Warsaw in 1934, at sixty-three, he possessed the bearing of a much younger man. In addition to Polish, Zeyde spoke several languages, but not English. So, when he arrived, it was agreed that Yiddish, the language of Eastern European Jews, would be our means of communication with him. In time, we children caught on to the language and came to know our grandfather well.

Although our home was observant and immersed in Jewish ritual, it wasn't until Zeyde arrived that I came to experience a *yiddishkeit,* or Jewishness, that warms the soul. And what a joy it was to have my grandpa in the house! There was a piety about him, a gentleness that made the Judaism he practiced feel warm and inviting.

Shlomo Tzvi Garbarz (1871–1946)

People don't often recognize that Judaism is as much a tradition of storytelling as it is of laws. I remember Zeyde telling us a *midrash* (story from the rabbis) about Abraham, the biblical father of the Jewish people. The midrash goes like this:

As a boy, Abraham visits the idol-making shop of his father, Terach. Abraham is furious that Terach is promoting idolatry and, while Terach is out of the shop, he smashes every idol statue there with a hammer, except one. He then places the hammer in the hands of that last untouched idol. Upon returning to his shop, Terach asks his son what has happened. Abraham responds that the largest idol has smashed the rest.

In his consternation, Terach says, "That's impossible! Idols are made of but wood and stone." To which Abraham replies, "Then why do you worship them and encourage others to do so?" With this experience, Abraham leaves his father's home and starts on a path to believing in and worshipping the one true God. That is how Jewish monotheism was born.

"Can you find this story in the Torah for me?" Zeyde asked.

"Of course!" we said, certain that our scholarship would please our grandfather. However, search though we did, we could not find the story. How could that be? We all knew the midrash, having been taught it since we were small.

"If it is not found in the Torah, then how do we know of these things?" Zeyde asked us. We could not answer him, but his smile was reassuring. "Not everything we know about our history is written in the Torah." He took delight in telling us about the Oral Law and the stories of the rabbis.

Equally gifted with his hands, Zeyde was a true artisan who crafted exquisite pieces of furniture. Upon arriving in Dublin, he began to build us a much-needed dining table, fashioned from mahogany, with extra leaves to seat fourteen people. That proved to be an absolute necessity during the war years, when we housed so many guests and refugees. From tables and cabinets to bookcases with sliding glass doors, Zeyde made them all for us (even a toilet seat carved from mahogany!).

One summer morning at breakfast, when I was about nine or ten, Ma complained of not having a refrigerator and a pantry large enough to store food for her growing family of seven. In those days, a fridge was not a common item in homes; daily trips to the butcher or grocer were the shopping norm. Zeyde was especially quiet during this talk. Stroking his beard, his eyes distant, no one realized that he was taking special note of Ma's complaint.

An hour or so later, I heard a digging noise coming from the yard. Looking out from my bedroom window, I saw Zeyde standing in a hole, wielding a shovel.

"What are you doing, Zeyde?"

"What does it look like I'm doing?"

"Digging a hole."

He looked up at me and nodded. "Good boy."

I watched for a moment longer. "But Zeyde, why are you digging a hole?"

"Why do you think?"

I shrugged my shoulders. "I don't know."

"Come here, *boychick*," he said, motioning for me to come down. . .

The hole was three feet deep. I looked on in fascination as worms moved in and out of the dirt walls; beetles and bugs scurried for cover, out of reach from the piercing shovelhead. Zeyde leaned his shovel aside and lifted me into the hole.

"Touch the dirt at the bottom," he said.

I pressed my hand against the cool, moist earth.

"What do you notice?"

"It's cold."

He smiled. "That's right. Clever boy." He lifted me out of the hole and set me on the ground.

"But what is the hole for?" I asked him again, puzzled.

"It's colder in the ground," he said, not giving away its purpose.

He continued digging until the hole was about six feet deep and never answered my question. He left it for me to figure out – the best kind of teaching. The next day he bought a large metal drum, and I watched in amazement as Zeyde built a wooden frame around it, with a door and cover.

"Now what are you doing, Zeyde?"

"I can't have your mother climb into a hole every time she needs something, can I?"

By the time he was done, he had constructed a pulley system with a three-shelved round contraption that could easily be raised above ground and lowered with a rope. "That's it then," he said. He was finished.

Our mother brought out milk and food: meats, cheeses, and vegetables, and Zeyde placed them on the three shelves inside the drum and showed Ma how to use the pulley system.

"None of it will go bad now," he smiled. She hugged and kissed him with thankfulness and shouted, "What a *mechayeh* (pleasure)!"

Indeed, Zeyde had fashioned a homemade refrigerator. A simple and clever mechanical design, he shared his invention with our friends and neighbors, so they too could benefit from his ingenuity.

Though accomplished at many things, Zeyde had no formal education. His carpentry and craft, including that of cabinetmaker, were learned in apprenticeship, which doesn't quite explain his ear for music. He once carved a violin out of wood for me and tuned it to pitch, without needing to hear the 'A' note from the piano.

"How did you do that?!" I asked, astonished that tuning could be perfected without a piano.

He tapped his forehead. "From the head, boychick, from the head."

More than a Renaissance man, Zeyde was truly a *tzaddik,* a wise and righteous human being. There is folklore among religious Jews that, in every generation, thirty-six *tzaddikim* (righteous spirits) walk the earth, and upon them rest the burdens of the world. Because of his patient wisdom, kindness, and gentle nature, there were whispers in our community: *Do you think Shlomo Garbarz could be a lamed vav (one of the thirty-six)?* Neighbors and friends held him in high esteem.

* * *

Zeyde, Rachel, and Theo (1944)

Now, the passing of a tzaddik is a moment of considerable note. Zeyde's death seemed to underline his holiness in an uncanny way. His health began to decline in the summer of 1946. What started as a cold settled into his chest. He was weak and running a fever. Even in the summer, my mother had steam in his room, trying to loosen the congestion in his lungs.

"Zeyde, are you all right?" I would ask him.

He would smile at me and nod his head. "Of course, *mein kint* (my child)."

But a moment later, he would be struck with fits of coughing. The deep congestion rattling in his lungs frightened me.

"Stop worrying," my mother would say, as she ferried cup after cup of hot tea to my grandfather, urging him to drink. But I couldn't stop worrying, nor could anyone else.

Soon, we had the doctor over, and he gave Zeyde a thick syrup to try and loosen the phlegm. For a couple of days, he improved but then fell ill again and, during the next months, became progressively weaker. He was pale and drawn. His skin had a waxy feel to it. Zeyde rarely joined us at meals, but when he did, it was like a holiday. His condition was grave; he seemed to be shrinking into himself.

Toward the end of summer, the doctor visited every day. A pall descended on our family, and the community expressed its concern. At the onset of the High Holy Days, late September, Zeyde's condition had deteriorated to the point where he could not come to shul for Rosh Hashanah.

Rosh Hashanah, literally the "head of the year," begins the holiest season in the Jewish calendar – the day on which God created

Adam and Eve, the last and most precious of His creations. So, according to tradition, Rosh Hashanah is the birthday of humankind.

At this important time, Jews reaffirm their desire to maintain a close relationship with God, to observe His commandments and to serve Him throughout their lives. God reviews the status of His Creation and determines whether each of us merits another year in the world.

At the sounding of the *shofar* (ram's horn), the "Book of Life" is opened. Every Jew has the next ten days to engage in *teshuva* (repentance and introspection) to determine if he or she will be inscribed in that book before the conclusion of Yom Kippur.

There can be no doubt to the solemnity of this time in the Jewish calendar. The High Holydays draw even the least religious into synagogues, where they are instilled with a sense of awe and holiness. Religious Jews stand literally quaking in judgment before the throne of God, asking forgiveness.

At the conclusion of prayer services on the first night of Rosh Hashanah, Jews offer a special greeting to one another, commemorating the holiday's importance: "May you be inscribed and sealed for a good year." That is, may your name be written in the Book of Life.

Zeyde taught me that repentance is not simply a question of asking God for forgiveness. He would say, "God can only grant forgiveness if He has been sinned against directly. Our rabbis teach that for God to forgive you for harming another person, you must first make amends with him or her." It's customary for Jews to seek out others they have wronged during the year and ask their forgiveness.

Teshuvah requires genuine regret for the past and an honest commitment to the future. Even the most pious Jew seeks the opportunity to stand trembling before God's throne during this season. From the time of his youth, my Zeyde had never missed a Rosh Hashanah service. But that year, it was impossible for him to attend.

He turned his face from me, hiding his tears. "You say the prayers for me as well, Theo," he said.

"I will, Zeyde. I will."

I don't believe I've ever said my prayers as fervently as I did on that Rosh Hashanah, with the image of Zeyde in my mind. Still, his condition worsened over the next ten days. Zeyde looked so much older than his seventy-six years. However, when Yom Kippur arrived, he could not be dissuaded from attending shul for the Kol Nidre evening service, the holiest night of the year.

"Zeyde, you can't!" my mother said.

He steeled himself with quiet dignity and said, "I have not missed Kol Nidre in all my life. I will attend."

Yom Kippur is a "fasting" holyday, during which food and water are prohibited for twenty-four hours. However, Judaism values human life and health above all else. With this in mind, weak or infirmed people are allowed to drink and eat, lest they faint or become ill during the services. Given my Zeyde's righteous nature, we knew his intention would be to fast through the entire day.

"Zeyde, I'm worried about you," I said.

He gave a brief smile, the twinkle, which had always lit his eyes, was gone. "Please," he said firmly.

We helped Zeyde into his best *yom tov* (holyday) suit and tie, and I walked with him to the shul. This Kol Nidre evening fell on the Jewish Sabbath. It was a most awesome intersection of sacred times. As we walked, his hand holding my arm, I could feel his weakness. He had lost considerable weight, and his slender frame was now almost ghostly. His eyes seemed already to be gazing at the world to come. He leaned heavily on my arm as we walked across the road to the shul.

In the eyes of neighbors, I could see love and concern for my zeyde. Few had seen him recently as he was confined to the house. Even as he nodded greetings to the many well-wishers who approached him, I could not imagine how Zeyde would make it through the evening prayers and Yom Kippur day, without food or water.

"Are you all right, Zeyde?"

He let his eyes close for a moment and smiled, not saying a word. But I had my answer. Whatever else could be said, I knew that Zeyde was where he needed to be this Kol Nidre evening.

We entered the shul, filled to capacity and spilling out into the courtyard. The men stood in their pews on the ground floor of the sanctuary, the women, in the balcony above; each turned to their neighbor wishing them *g'mar chatimah tovah*. (May you be sealed in the Book of Life.)

I could see my father in his white silken *kitel* (robe) and white hat, making his way to the bimah, from where he would chant the "Kol Nidre" – a haunting introduction to the evening service. The air was electric with anticipation. This was one of the singular moments in my father's life as a chazzan. With the chanting of "Kol Nidre," he intended to open the hearts of all who came to pray that night. A three-hour evening service would be followed by an additional eight hours the next day – a marathon of prayer, conducted without food or water, that called upon both his physical and spiritual strength.

As a signal that the Kol Nidre would begin, a shul official opened the doors to the *aron hakodesh* (holy ark) revealing the sacred Torah scrolls. A hush fell. . .

Greenville Hall Synagogue (1925-1985)
"Bimah Table, Aron Hakodesh & Torah Scrolls"

Just as the Book of Life is opened on Rosh Hashanah, it is sealed for the coming year with the final blast of the shofar, heard at the conclusion of Yom Kippur. I could sense Zeyde's resolve to hear that shofar blow again. We walked along the pews past many who reached out to touch him gently on the shoulder, as if he were a holy object commanding their deepest respect.

I held his hand as we moved directly in front of the ark. Three Torahs sat in white velvet dress, crowned in silver, as kings upon their thrones; proud breastplates and shimmering ornaments adorned them. Zeyde paused for a long moment, his eyes fixed on these bastions of light. I felt him squeeze my hand tightly, and then, slowly. . . slowly, he sank down to the floor.

A cry from the balcony and, in a moment, several doctors in the congregation rushed to Zeyde's side. "Give him room!" one shouted. "Loosen his shirt and tie," said another. But nothing could be done for him – it was his time. My grandfather had passed to the *olam habah*, the world to come, on the holiest night of the year.

Tears flowed that Kol Nidre night for Shlomo Tzvi Garbarz and for the Garb family. A small group of men carried my zeyde across the street to our home and laid him gently on the dining room floor. We placed lit candles at his feet and by his head. As tradition dictates, a *shomer* (watcher) was found who would stay with him and recite the Psalms of David until the time of his burial. (Jewish law forbids a body to be left alone.)

From the bimah, my father had witnessed Zeyde's collapse and immediately went into silent prayer, beseeching God to save his father's life. As Zeyde was carried from the sanctuary, Da raised his eyes to the heavens, choking back tears. Though emotionally drained, not wanting to disappoint the congregation, he asked that he be allowed to continue as chazzan and begin the Kol Nidre prayer.

"It will be an honor for me to complete the service for my father," he said, looking over to where the council members were seated.

The Council granted his request. Many in the congregation wept openly throughout the service as my father's emotions gave each prayer a meaning that was utterly transcendent. If you ask anyone today, still alive, they will tell you how especially poignant and beautiful Wolf's chanting was on this night.

It was later we discovered that the clock, which sat on the fireplace mantle in Zeyde's bedroom, stopped at the exact moment of his passing. We also learned that my Uncle David, a cantor in Blackpool, England, at the time, had experienced a choking spasm during his service at the very same moment and was unable to continue for an hour.

After the funeral in the Dolphin's Barn Cemetery, I heard people from the congregation speak of my zeyde as a tzaddik. There were discussions about the timing of his death. After all, it was considered a sign of righteousness to leave this world on Shabbos, and to do so on the Sabbath of Sabbaths was truly extraordinary. That he died on Yom Kippur was, in the eyes of many, a sign of Divine intervention.

There were those who expected to see an aura appear over him, as predicted by the mystical belief in the lamed vav. These speculations were communicated in whispers of genuine awe, testament to the love and reverence the community felt for Zeyde.

To me, my grandfather was not a prophet or an angel, but rather, flesh and blood, a man whom I loved dearly and who loved us, his family.

My father observed the seven-day *Shiva* (mourning) period with a brooding sadness. He was much affected by the circumstances of Zeyde's passing: "I was shocked and angry with Hashem at first," he said later, recalling the moment of his father's death, life leaving him in an instant, no goodbyes. "But now I understand that such a passing could only be a gift from God. Imagine, to leave this Earth while in shul, standing before the aron kodesh, on the holiest night of the year. That," he said with certainty, "is the greatest blessing any man could receive."

לזכרון אבינו היקר והנעלה
ירא ה' כל ימיו
ה"ה שלמה צבי בן אברהם ז"ל
נפטר בשם טוב גדול
ערב יום כפור תש"ז לפ"ק
בן ע"ז שנה לחייו
לדאבון לב בניו ובנותיו
ת נ צ ב ה

SOLOMON H. GARBARZ,
WHO DIED
ON THE EVE OF YOM KIPPUR
5707.

Gravestone of Solomon Hersch Garbarz
Dolphins Barn Cemetery, Dublin, Ireland

155

Chapter 20
The Disappearance

Like every family in Dublin's Jewish community, the Garb family's personal drama was set against a much larger stage. History was being written with the continuing struggle to establish the State of Israel. It would take the near destruction of European Jewry for the dream of a Jewish state to be realized. During and after the war, our community followed every bit of news related to the British Mandate in Palestine.

On July 22, 1946, in response to multiple British raids on Jewish agencies in Palestine, and in defiance of Britain's control over the land, the Zionist group, Irgun, blew up the British Administration Headquarters in Jerusalem. Known as the "King David Hotel Bombing," this attack, which had been called off (but too late to relay the message), killed ninety-three people and injured dozens more. *The Manchester Guardian* argued that "British firmness inside Palestine has brought about more terrorism and has worsened the situation in the country – the opposite effect that the government had intended." (Wikipedia)

During this period, Jewish leaders began a *ha'apala* (illegal immigration) using small boats operating in total secrecy. With the protection of the *Palmach* (elite fighting force of the *Haganah,* the underground army of the Jewish community), tens of thousands of Jews came into Palestine between 1946 and 1947, in this way. Many others were captured and imprisoned by the British.

It is a terrible irony that the British, in policing the Middle East, posed the greatest threat to Jews who longed to enter The Promised Land. The British Mandate, which traced back to the 1917 Balfour Declaration, clearly held that a Jewish state should be founded.

"But when?" we kept asking. In the numbness and chaos following World War II, that was the question that aroused our passion.

"There will be a Jewish state," my brother said with assurance.

"That's what everyone is saying," I said.

"But it won't just happen."

"What do you mean?"

"We have to *make* it happen. We can't sit around waiting for others to bring it about."

I listened to Abe with interest, having rarely heard him speak with such Zionist passion. While he studied at Trinity College, emissaries from Palestine and Britain visited there and spoke of the need for volunteers to help build the future land of Israel. Fighters as well as farmers were needed.

Meanwhile, by the fall of 1947, a civil war was brewing between the Jews and the Arabs living in Palestine. If the State of Israel were born, the Arab nations vowed to drive the Jews into the sea. The situation was spiraling out of control, when the British announced that they would end their mandate and withdraw by May 1948. This decision threw Palestine into a state of ethnic and civil unrest. A full-scale war appeared to be on the horizon.

One Shabbos morning at Kiddush, early summer, 1947, Abe pulled me aside for a *shehakol* (a toast). His expression was dynamic, his eyes, blazing. With chilling conviction, he looked right through me and said, "It's time to make Israel a reality." And then he was gone...

That evening as we gathered for dinner, Da looked up and asked, "Where's Abey?" No one knew. He was usually home for the meal, unless he said otherwise. "That's Abey for you," my father said under his breath.

My mother shushed him. "You'll only have trouble with your pressure," she said, trying her best to make the meal pleasant.

After dinner, Lucy tickled the ivories. As on so many evenings, I sat in the living room and closed my eyes, enjoying her repertoire of Chopin, Schubert, and Bach. I took great pleasure in her playing, though I do remember times that I'd awaken late at night to musical scales and bang my shoe on the floor to silence her practice. On this night, we all enjoyed her playing, unconcerned with Abe's absence. Da was annoyed with him, that's all. He might have been studying, or perhaps out with friends or a young lady.

Da's annoyance turned to concern when Abe failed to come home that night. From his demeanor, it was clear that his non-presence was not open for discussion. But when he didn't return the next day, or the next, fears about his well-being consumed my family.

* * *

Theo and Abe, Dublin, Ireland (1947)

Abey's disappearance was the prelude to our father's darkest season. Not only had he lost his beloved father, but his elder son was missing, and a long time would pass before his fate was known. Adding to his difficulties, my father was confronted with shameful events at the synagogue that would ultimately cause him to resign his position.

Being a member of the clergy is not an easy task, because of the higher standards to which one is held, in addition to making oneself available to congregation members at all hours. There is also the Jewish tradition of "welcoming the guest," a custom of providing hospitality, extending back to Abraham and Sarah.

As leaders of the community, it is incumbent upon rabbis and cantors to fully support these traditions. Years ago, they were not paid very much for their service to God and community and were strapped with financial burdens beyond their meager salaries.

My father reached a point where he was concerned not only with our day-to-day living expenses, but with his ability to provide for our future. Accordingly, he looked to diversify his income. Thanks to Ma's family in Belgium, the foundation for a small trade in jewelry had existed for years. Da began to expand on this idea and, as well, started a fur trading business, operating small cottage factories.

Taking another fork in the road, he and Lucy established a national driving school – the O'Connell Bridge School of Motoring – I believe the first of its kind in Ireland, in that it prompted Eire to initiate a standardized testing and licensing of drivers. Before this, one could send away in the mail for a driver's license. As crazy as it sounds, I did so in my dog's name and, a few weeks later, received a license for him to drive both automatic and manual transmissions! The driving school would also influence my personal life. Indeed, it would open a whole new chapter for me.

Da's enterprises flourished, and the Council at Greenville Hall would typically look away, as side businesses enabled clergy to support their families without necessitating salary increases. However, Chazzan Garb's success began to draw the ire of board members, who were prominent doctors, lawyers, and business owners in the community. Those in the diamond trade alleged that our family's jewelry business was in competition with their own, and this they would not permit. They protested: "Chazzan Garb is in breach of his contract!"

Now, given that family members ran each enterprise, with Da acting strictly as adviser, I found their objections baseless. My father was well-aware of his contract terms and conducted his affairs with utmost discretion.

Another concern of the board had to do with Da's role as *sheliach tzibbur* (messenger of God). The Council was debating whether his voice could be heard on the world stage, or was it only to be used as an instrument of prayer? Did these men have the right to deny him a role in the opera or theatre? Well evidently, they thought so, and their brooding continued.

My father had always been involved in music beyond the synagogue; he sang both opera and liturgical song in concerts for Jewish charities. From the time we came to Dublin, he had pursued formal voice training at the Irish Conservatory of Music. His mentor, Professor Viani of Italy, offered him the lead role in *Pagliacci,* with the Dublin Operatic Society.

This was a great honor and my father was thrilled at the prospect. Not only would his singing talents be acknowledged in the secular arts, it was an opportunity Da relished as a performer.

Late one evening close to midnight, there was a knock on our front door. Was it the police bringing news of Abe's disappearance? I ran to the top of the stairs and saw my father breathe in deeply and sigh heavily before opening the door.

In front of Da stood two council members from the synagogue with a serious look on their faces. "Chazzan Garb, sorry for disturbing you so late at night. There is an emergency board meeting called for midnight, and you are requested to attend."

I guess no news was good news when it came to Abe. As for my father, he brought news to the dinner table the following evening that left a bitter taste in our mouths, despite Ma's delicious strawberry rhubarb compote.

"Rachel, may I tell you about the shul's emergency that they dragged me out of bed for?" I could see the hurt in his eyes. "The board has learned of our family enterprise, Diamond Gem Setters, and they are insisting either that we stop trading in diamonds, or that I resign my position as cantor of Greenville Hall," he said, pounding his fist on the table.

At this, Sarah, now twelve, dropped her head and began sobbing, a faint whimper, that brought our emotions to the surface. I was disgusted with the shul and saddened for Da. What else could happen to the Garbs this year?

"Oh, my dearest Wolf! Why are diamonds of such importance to them?" Ma said.

"You see, my rose (as he often called her), a few of these men are in the diamond business, themselves, and do not wish for us to be in competition with them. And this is not all." His voice became quiet and wistful, "They have heard of my audition for the lead in Pagliacci and have asked me to pass on it. The Council will not allow their chazzan to perform secular music – only prayer."

With this, Da stood and began to chant a soulful rendition of "Eitz Chayim Hi." (The Torah, It is a tree of life.) We listened, our tears flowing, joining together for the last few words: *chadesh yameinu kekedem.* (Renew our lives as in days of old.) He turned and, looking me straight in the eye, said bitterly, "Children, never get involved in a congregational business. The shul board will tear your *kishkes* out."

The hostility engendered by this midnight "witch hunt" continued. This led to a synagogue tribunal empowered to review my father's contract and to question his activities. I recall it played out as a "kangaroo court" with the Council intent on placing Chazzan Garb under its thumb.

Initially, my father was determined to address the issues and clear his name. But as time passed, it was obvious that staying on as cantor would keep him from performing on the world stage and, as well, supervising our family's businesses.

And so, during the summer of 1947, he tendered his resignation to Greenville Hall Synagogue. I don't believe that was the outcome the shul board envisioned, but it was soon a *fait accompli* and a disconcerting time for my family. Our position in the community was well-established. To witness him endure this treatment and then leave the shul challenged our sense of belonging.

Thank God our discomfort was short-lived. While he was unappreciated by the Council, others in Dublin's Jewish community did not ignore my father's worth. Within days, he received an offer to serve as cantor of the Lennox Road Synagogue, in Dublin.

There, he was to enjoy a freedom that he had never experienced. Not only was he allowed to perform on stage with Dublin's Jewish Dramatic Society, he took advantage of an invitation to visit the United States, where he auditioned among fifty cantors for a position at a prominent Conservative synagogue, Mishkan Tefila, in Boston, Massachusetts. Da was hired and led high holyday services there in the fall of 1947 and sang on a number of live Yiddish radio broadcasts.

In February of the following year, he returned to Dublin with many things to tell about America – stories that stirred my imagination and my dreams of traveling abroad. I still marvel at one of the items my father brought back from the States – a copy of *Esquire* magazine! I never did learn how he had evaded the Irish censors.

* * *

CONGREGATION MISHKAN TEFILA

SEAVER STREET at ELM HILL AVE. — BOSTON 21, MASS.

March 8, 1948

To Whom It May Concern:

This is to certify that Cantor Wolf Garbarz of Dublin, Ireland, officiated at the High Holiday Services at our main Temple, which has a seating capacity of over 1800.

Cantor Garbarz was chosen from a list of over fifty candidates whom we auditioned for the position. After the Holiday Services, our Board of Directors voted unanimously to engage him as our permanent cantor to succeed our late beloved cantor, Izao G. Glickstein, who served us for a period of twenty-five years. However, due to possible delays in Cantor Garbarz' obtaining a permanent visa to remain in the United States and also to the possibility that we might not obtain the services of another cantor on whom we had an eye, if it turned out that a visa for Cantor Garbarz could not be had, we engaged this other cantor. However, since we signed our contract with this other cantor, we found a formula by which Cantor Garbarz could very easily obtain a permanent visa.

As Vice-President of the Congregation and Chairman of the Cantorial Committee, I am pleased to state that, in my humble opinion, Cantor Garbarz has no peer in the American Cantorate. He is gifted with a beautiful dramatic tenor voice of unusual range and quality. He is a pious Jew who fears God and may truly be called an "Ish Yehudi". When one gets to know him intimately, one will find in him the genuine "Sheliach Teibur", a personality who is worthy to be a true messenger of his people. He is a great Hebrew scholar, whose "Parush Hamilus" is "par excellence". His "Nusach Hatfilah" is the truly traditional Jewish "Nusach" and is not the kind of "Nusach" based on operatic or other foreign sources.

I feel certain that after one meets Cantor Garbarz and one gets fully acquainted with him and one listens to his inimitable renditions of our sacred chants, one will find that I have understated rather than overstated his true worth.

B. LEONARD KOLOVSON
Vice-President, Congregation
Chairman, Cantorial Committee

"In my humble opinion, Cantor Garbarz has no peer in the American Cantorate. He is gifted with a beautiful dramatic tenor voice of unusual range and quality… a personality worthy to be a true messenger of his people. After one… listens to his inimitable renditions of our sacred chants, one will find that I have understated, rather than overstated, his true worth."

During this period, Da continued his efforts on behalf of the World Zionist Organization. As is well known, the quest for a Jewish homeland has had a long history. For centuries, the dream of Zion was not far from the hearts of Jews all over the world. My father worked as hard as any man to bring this dream to fruition.

On May 14, 1948, the dream became a reality when Israel raised her flag and declared statehood. After nearly two thousand years of Diaspora, Israel became a nation once again! The Jewish people had regained their homeland, *Eretz Yisrael* (the land of Israel).

Upon hearing the news, my family was among the thousands of Dublin Jews who celebrated. We gathered around the radio to hear the broadcast of David Ben Gurion as he read the Declaration of Statehood. Oh, how we sang and danced! I don't believe I ever saw my father as emotional with joy as he was that day. He embraced each of us with tears streaming down his face. His voice crackled with delight. "Finally! Finally!!" he shouted.

Like so many families, we enjoyed our private celebration and then headed down to O'Connell Street. There was no organized decision to gather there, but we knew it was the place to be. We spontaneously joined the massive, jubilant circle and danced the "Hora," singing *"Am Yisrael Chai."* (The nation of Israel lives.) As the circle grew, we broke off and formed circles within circles and continued dancing in a spirited victory party.

Much of Irish Dublin celebrated with us. It wasn't that they shared in our joy of founding a Jewish State. They viewed it as a defeat for the British Empire, something the Irish will always raise a glass to.

Our *simcha* (joy) escalated to the raucous merriment Irish revelers fondly call "hooley." Of course, no one forgot the awful price paid for our deliverance to come. Thousands of years of persecution, and, in our generation alone, six million Jewish souls paid the ultimate sacrifice for Israel's redemption.

In the weeks to come, we would learn of Abey's fate. Nearly a year had passed without word. The police investigation was fruitless. It was a great mystery, as we learned that several Jewish families across Ireland had experienced the same heartache and bewilderment, their sons too disappearing in the middle of the night. Had they been kidnapped? Were they still alive?

We remained hopeful, until the day a letter arrived to our home. It was postmarked "Israel," addressed to the Garb family, and appeared to be in Abe's handwriting. Da sat at the dining room table and ran his fingers over the envelope as we gathered around. Could it be a letter from Abe?

There was never a reply to all those letters my parents wrote to family members in Poland and Belgium, during the war. But now, a letter, seemingly from beyond the pale. My father opened the envelope and held the sheaf of papers, his hands trembling. Thirteen pages written in Abe's handwriting!

To us, it was a miracle, and what a story the letter told! My brother had arrived in the Holy Land with a small group of Irish, Jewish young men. Their mission? To join the fight in liberating Israel from both the British and the Arabs. Although the story is now familiar, with books and movies portraying the modern "Exodus" of Jews to a land known as Palestine, my brother's account was fresh and thrilling to experience.

In his letter, Abe apologized for causing us worry. He explained that secrecy was demanded of him before and well after leaving Ireland – especially family members were not to know of the worldwide volunteer effort, as they were likely to dissuade their sons from leaving and, in the process, endanger others. "I had no choice but to comply," he wrote.

As my father read the letter, he nodded, "Of course, of course, I understand." The story that unfolded enthralled us: although a student doctor at the time, the needs of the freedom fighters were so great that he was called upon to be an assistant surgeon. He described the fighting, but not in terms that would upset our mother. Rather, he wrote of the bravery of the young Jewish men and women with whom he served, and of their shared faith that God was with them in their fight. He spoke of the lush countryside and the magic of setting his eyes upon *Yerushalayim shel Zahav* (Jerusalem of Gold), for the first time.

Our Abey would be one of many heroes in the war for Israel's independence, which began the day after Israel raised her flag (in compliance with the United Nations Partition Plan, dividing Palestine into a Jewish and Arab state). Over the next year, his letters came often and our family read each one with tremendous pride. "It's so dangerous," my mother would gasp. But even in her worry, she could not hide the love and pride she felt for her courageous son.

I was nineteen and mused at the thought of my brother choosing a noble and heroic path on behalf of the Jewish people. Who could have imagined it? Truthfully, we feared that he would be a prisoner of his folly. Instead, the prodigal son had redeemed himself.

And what path would I choose, now entering Trinity College and mingling with the Irish? Remain true to my faith and my parents' wishes? Or follow my heart, wherever it might lead. . .

Chapter 21

Margaret

Life went on for us in Dublin much as it had before, but with the future of Israel in mind. I was studying economics and business administration at Trinity College and, as well, acting in plays there. However, at nineteen, a good deal of my psychic energy focused on budding Irish lasses.

Many were the nights my friends and I went to dances and parties despite a heavy load of schoolwork. We frequented local hotspots such as the Four Provinces Dance Hall and the Crystal Ballroom.

I worked in our family's driving school, which gave me a unique advantage when it came to romance: a car parked in our garage was at my disposal. But how to sneak out of the house undetected – that was the thing. More times than I can remember, I would climb out of my bedroom window onto the roof, jump to the ground and "borrow" a car to meet my date. On occasion, I collected my latest love outside her church, just after she confessed her carnal sins from our prior encounter.

"Do you ever confess to sins you have yet to commit?" I once asked.

"Don't be presumptuous," she said, and slapped me playfully.

I enjoyed the company of these young women and was honest with them in saying that we could never be more than lovers.

"Why not?"

"I'm Jewish."

"What does that have to do with anything?"

"I can only marry a Jewish girl."

"Well, I'm supposed to marry a Catholic boy, but so what? A cousin of mine married outside of the Church. There were a few tears, but they got over it."

"It would be a big deal in my family," I said. "They'd *never* get over it."

Then I would patiently explain how we were taught from childhood that Jewish law forbids marriage between a Jew and a Gentile. Most of the girls would understand and continue seeing me.

I also dated Jewish girls, one seriously, but sexual taboos doomed those relationships, and I was too young to think of marriage. On the other hand, my romances with Catholic girls flourished but could not be sustained either.

Despite it all, I was having the time of my life! I paid no mind to the dangers of the game I was playing. My cocksure behavior was founded on naiveté. Little did I know that I would soon fall in love with someone of a different faith.

My lesson came in the form of one of the loveliest women I have ever known – her name, Margaret. She was a gorgeous nineteen-year-old with light brown hair and liquid brown eyes. When I saw her for the first time, I was stunned into uncharacteristic silence by her beauty. *She's far too beautiful for me,* I thought.

Margaret entered our school of motoring one day in April 1949. "I'm here for driving lessons," she said, her eyes gleaming. Not only was this girl fabulous, she was half a head taller than me. She leaned in closer, expectantly.

"Yes, well, lovely then," I said. "Ready to get on the road?"

"What? I'm going to drive immediately?"

I laughed. "Isn't that why you're here?"

"But I've never –"

"Don't worry, trust me."

After she filled out the required paperwork, I walked her to a car, opened the driver-side door, and motioned for her to get in, taking the passenger seat for myself. I laid the key in her hand and told her to start the engine.

She looked at me curiously, so I reached over and, placing my hand on hers, guided the key into the ignition. She smiled at me and my heart began pounding. I was smitten!

Until that day, the first lesson was always the same: sitting in the car with the pupil in the driver's seat. They would be taught the rules of the road, how to shift gears, and to read the dials. Operating the stick shift and clutch was the greatest challenge for new drivers and, in this regard, Margaret was typical.

Nevertheless, she drove a bit, and then I took the wheel, and we chatted away as if we had known each other for some time. "That was lovely," she said, getting out of the car. "Do you think I'll get the hang of it?"

"I'm sure you will."

"I was nervous at first."

I nodded, "Everyone is."

"But you were right." I looked at her, puzzled. She smiled and said, "I mean you told me to trust you and everything would be okay. So, you were right."

There was an electricity between us that both excited and troubled me. As our next lesson drew near, I panicked and assigned her another instructor, but she threatened to quit unless I stayed the course. I thought about it, and, as they say in business, "the customer is always right." So, as a good businessman, naturally, I agreed to continue with our lessons, though my reluctance caught my sister Lucy's attention. "It's not as if she has fangs. She's delightful and pretty too. I can't believe you, Theo."

After our second lesson, I looked forward to each session with a mixture of excitement and dread. We discovered that we shared a love for classical music and often hummed melodies together. Now and then, she would glance over at me with an alluring smile. Oh, I was falling fast!

"You must have a lot of girls asking after you."

I was surprised and flattered she would think so.

"Not as many as the boys chasing after you," I said, trying to sound casual.

She laughed, and then her smile faded. "I don't find many of the boys I meet very interesting."

In a way, Margaret was easier to talk to than other girls; she was different. My attraction for her was more than physical, and this scared me. At first, I thought her interest was in polite conversation but, with each meeting, I sensed her feelings for me grow. It was the way she laughed or challenged me with an observation I made about music or art. She encouraged me to place my hand on hers when she grappled with the stick shift – something was brewing...

The weather was lovely that time of year, and she often lowered her window as we drove, causing her auburn hair to blow wildly in the breeze. I would turn and study the outline of her face... she was perfection. When she looked back at me, I would direct her attention to the road. "The last thing we need is to have an accident."

"Oh, but you wouldn't let us get into a wreck," she said, flirting with me.

Maybe not with the car, but I had the distinct feeling we were heading toward another kind of wreck. The day of her final lesson came, and I was almost relieved.

During this session, Margaret turned to me and said, "You know, I think you're the best friend I've made in a very long time."

"You, as well." Alarm bells were sounding in my head; I was hesitant to suggest that our friendship continue. A few times she mentioned pictures playing at this or that cinema, or a concert that I might enjoy and, at one point, asked rather boldly, "Do you ever go out with Irish girls?"

I breathed in deeply. "On occasion."

She perked up. "Then might you want to go out with me sometime?"

"Well, you're a student. It wouldn't be right." *A rather lame excuse, and she knew it!*

"That's ridiculous," she said, annoyed with me. And then she was silent.

Margaret was a fast learner and became a competent driver before her eight hours of instruction ended. For a novice, she seemed relaxed behind the wheel.

"I've done it right, then?" she asked.

"Perfectly, congratulations. You truly are one of the best students I've ever taught." I extended my hand to wish her luck and, as we shook, she leaned in and wrapped her other arm around my neck.

"Thank you," she said softly, planting a warm kiss on my cheek. How delicious! I was walking on a cloud for the rest of the day.

Theo Garb, O'Connell Bridge School of Motoring (1953)

Saddened, yet relieved, I thought Margaret was out of my life. However, a few weeks later, she returned, saying that she needed additional lessons to feel comfortable behind the wheel. "I don't want to be one of those timid drivers who crawl along the road on the way to the shops." Margaret insisted I be her instructor, announcing to all that she'd have no other than Theo.

Early in this next round of lessons, she asked if I would go to the cinema with her.

"I would love to, but I can't."

"Can't?"

"I come from a very religious family. I –"

"But you've been out with other Irish girls."

I was silent for a moment, then nodded my head and tried to explain, "But a girl of your station in life –"

"Oh please," she said dismissively. "What difference does it make?"

Margaret was neither Jewish nor common. She was from a social status far above mine. Her family was wealthy and, as landed gentry, highly regarded in Irish society. She lived in the countryside and commuted by bus to her work in town.

Because of her social standing and being a Catholic, I knew that my feelings for her could only lead to trouble. I didn't know how to respond. "I go out with Irish girls to have some fun. It could never be more than that."

She laughed. "Theo, I like you very much and enjoy your company, but I'm asking you to go to the pictures with me, not marry me!"

I felt foolish and stammered, "B-but I didn't –"

"Theo, you're the first Jewish person I've ever spoken to. I didn't know what to expect. Someone with your love of music, cinema, and books – you enjoy all the things I do.

"That's true, but –"

"Now I know you like movies, and I think you like me, so it seems we ought to go." With her eyes burning mine, she added, "as friends."

Part of our electric chemistry no doubt came from our shared passion for the arts. I never gave it much thought, having grown up with that sensibility, but it occurred to me that the girls I dated had not shared those interests.

Unlike the Irish boys she knew, I was not a drinker. Margaret shared that, regardless of their upbringing, they became loutish when they drank, aggressive, and somewhat crude. And she was uncomfortable with that.

Our talks deepened and encompassed many topics: the arts, politics, social concerns, and family. She continued to hold that her interest was in friendship; she had found someone whom she could relate to. Despite my own joy in her company, I saw peril ahead. However, I could not bring myself to say goodbye; I cared for Margaret. Beautiful, intelligent, and full of life, she was everything this young man could want in a life partner – except Jewish.

I sensed her falling for me as well, and, looking to place distance between us, I once blurted out, "What do you want with a short Jewish boy anyway? We don't look a match and we have a completely different upbringing. There'd be nothing but heartache."

A child of privilege, Margaret dismissed my concerns. She came from a different world than I, a world I dare not trespass. Although our relationship grew intimate, I never set foot inside the tall gates that marked the entrance to her family's property. I could only peer at her mansion and gardens through those wrought iron bars and wonder: *to live in such a place, with such a girl!*

If ever there were a pair of dark Irish eyes that would not take no for an answer, by the time Margaret's second driving course ended, I agreed to go out with her.

"Strictly platonic," I said.

"Of course," she said, satisfied with her victory.

I invited her to see the picture, *Fantasia,* knowing its score would delight us both. We entered the darkened theatre and took seats in the back. As we watched the film, Margaret's hand found mine. Our fingers entwined and danced to the music. At one point, the conductor was describing the power of music, and I leaned over to whisper in her ear. She turned and our lips met in an innocent kiss. We looked at each other, longingly, and kissed again – a soft, sweet kiss. In that moment, I surrendered my heart to a thrilling and uncertain fate.

* * *

In the coming months, our relationship blossomed, a love affair kept secret from our families. The thought of my parents finding out and the pain this would cause them made each rendezvous with Margaret a guilt-laden pleasure. Covering for trysts with lies of schoolwork demands outside of home or being out with friends, I was soon living a life of deceit. In rare moments of clarity, I asked myself: *how could you risk everything for an affair that is doomed?*

With each encounter, my heart softened, and we grew closer. Our talks became more intimate and innocent kisses took on a passionate urgency. One evening while parked outside her estate, we gazed upon a night sky, black and clear. Stars were everywhere, tempting me to wish upon them. Oh, how I wished to find an answer to my inner torment!

I held Margaret's face gently in my hands and looked deeply into her eyes. My eyes said *I love you.* Her tears welled up, and we kissed, ever so tenderly. By the light of the moon, our bodies entwined in passionate lovemaking... The aching within us soothed, we held each other close for the longest time, then fixed our clothing, and Margaret, grabbing my shirt collar, kissed me hard on the mouth. I watched as she ran from the car and entered through the iron gates, which towered above us.

Margaret and I were careful never to be seen together in Dublin. Whether at the Abbey Theatre or in Phoenix Park, we arranged our meetings to look like chance encounters.

"What a surprise to see you here, Theo."

"Likewise. How's your driving coming along?"

"Splendid, thanks again."

"Oh yes," I said to a friend, who happened to be in the theatre on the same night, "Margaret took driving lessons with me at the O'Connell Bridge school. Funny to run into her like this."

Margaret was a high-spirited gal with a flair for the dramatic. She enjoyed the game more than I did, seeing how close we could be in public, without giving away our secret. We lived dangerously, actors in our own little play, not knowing how it would end. And we continued on with our affair.

On the occasions we met in public, at a concert or a film, we sat apart, embracing afterwards on a darkened side street, relishing these few chancy moments. There came a point that we couldn't stand the hiding, nor the discomfort of the automobile, and devised a ruse that would allow us to escape for a weekend away.

Just the two of us, we mused, *and no hiding*.

It sounded fabulous. To bring it off, we engaged the help of our closest friends; they were our cover, allowing us to get away. I chose a location where I was certain there would be no Jewish people. I could just imagine someone saying to my folks, "I saw Theo on the weekend in the countryside, with a lovely Irish girl."

Our first holiday together, we stole away to a little hotel in Drogheda. We rented two adjoining rooms because, to share a room, we would need proof of marriage. There was no way I could afford such a getaway and felt embarrassed that Margaret paid for us both. "Isn't being together more important than who pays?" she said – logic I couldn't refute.

The proprietor of the hotel gave us an inquisitive look upon arrival, but Margaret was her usual winning self and allayed whatever concerns he might have about us. We settled in, and, moments later, there was a tapping at the door connecting our rooms.

"Who is it?" I teased.

Margaret laughed and, as I opened the door, she fell into my arms. So began our glorious weekend alone, free to express our desires for one another without a care in the world. "Theo," she said, as we cuddled during the afternoon, "this is how it could be all the time."

I laughed. "Oh really? Perhaps in fantasyland."

She frowned, "Wouldn't you like to spend all of your time with me like this?"

That I could possess this woman was beyond my wildest dreams. I would have liked nothing more, but for the tormenting voice in my head: *If only she were Jewish. If only she were Jewish.*

* * *

During this romantic summer, we managed to get away with some frequency and visited the beautiful places in Ireland. Margaret and I shared a passion for horseback riding. She would lead two horses and twenty dogs from her father's stables and meet me outside the gates of her home. Many an afternoon, we rode in the lush, green, Irish hills, stopping along the way in hidden groves hospitable to our lovemaking.

On one of our outings, a little sports car came flying around the bend and spooked our horses, then screeched to a halt as the dogs filled the narrow country road. The driver jumped out to apologize. He was dark-skinned and quite handsome, as I remember, with piercing green eyes and a thin mustache.

"Sorry about that," he said. "I didn't think anyone was on the road." As he spoke, I could see that Margaret's beauty registered with him. "Magnificent horses! Give me your hand," he said, and helped her to dismount. I lowered myself to the ground, while observing their interaction.

"Hello, I'm Aly Khan. And you lovely, young people are?"

"I'm Theo and this is Margaret. Did you say your name is Aly Khan, as in Prince Aly Khan?" I asked, having heard of the famous playboy.

He gave a slight, graceful bow, his eyes fixed on Margaret; he was clearly taken with her. Aly had recently divorced his wife, and that he was a Muslim did not dissuade his interest in an Irish Catholic beauty – he was a ladies' man.

We stood in the road a few minutes and made small talk, after which, Margaret and I were ready to be on our way. The prince, however, was not anxious to let us go.

"You must come for dinner sometime," he said.

The invitation was directed at Margaret, though not overtly. "Theo, what do you think? Shall we?"

Who would pass on such an opportunity? "All right, then," I said. Aly looked at me, taking my measure, perhaps trying to gauge how a short, young lad had won over such a beauty.

"Smashing! It will be lovely to have you as my guests."

Naas, a town located twenty miles south and inland from Dublin, is where Margaret and I ventured to the following week. Known as horse country, Naas was one of the many residences of Prince Aly Kahn. He owned a villa and stables there, among other countries – France, Switzerland, and Venezuela – where he bred some of the finest racehorses in the world.

Aly's butler received us at the front door to his home. We walked into luxury as I had never encountered. The finest upholstered furniture, Persian rugs, silk draperies, marble columns and granite floors, crown moldings inlaid with gold, and fantastic paintings and sculpture. Prince Aly shouted greetings to us from the second-floor landing and hastened down the spiral staircase in a burgundy silk robe.

"So good to see you two," he said, shaking our hands. "Sorry for my dress. I got held up tending to Maggie, a sweet old mare with a sore foot. Robert, will you show my guests into the parlor. I shan't be long my dears, and again, my apologies."

Though twenty, I felt like a boy in Ali's company. A wealthy man of thirty-something, he had an air of sophistication and confidence about him. I admired these qualities and began to worry that our dinner invitation was a mistake. A man of this caliber could sweep Margaret off her feet before my eyes.

A few minutes later, Aly appeared wearing a dinner-jacket, shirt, and trousers. "Well then, may I offer you a drink? Some wine perhaps?"

The three of us reclined on plush couches, sipping a vintage bottle of red wine, toasting the end of summer. Aly shared with us his passion for racing sports cars, breeding derby-winning horses, and courting beautiful women.

At one point, Margaret left the room to powder her nose, and Aly, sitting opposite me, leaned in and spoke, "Your Margaret is quite a girl! She's beautiful, sharp, and with personality. Good for you, my boy." He sat back, sipped from his glass, and continued, "I'll tell you, I met a stunning redhead myself in Antibes last summer, and now we're married and expecting our first child. I imagine you read the papers. She's Rita Hayworth. The press calls her the 'Love Goddess,' and I have to say, she is all that, and more. Rita is home in Provence, taking it easy; the baby is due in December. I'm a lucky man, Theo. I wish the same for you." We raised our glasses and drank.

A sudden sense of relief passed through me, as I realized that my concerns were unfounded. However, there was one other detail to address about our evening together, and I was pleased that Margaret wasn't there to be bothered with it.

"Ali, I want you to know, by the way, that I'm Jewish, and I only eat kosher meat."

He laughed. "Don't worry, Theo. I'm Muslim, and you know, we Muslims slaughter animals in the same manner as do the Jews. All of our meat is kosher. However, I like fish and vegetarian foods myself. We'll have salmon. My chef is preparing a wonderful meal that you will both enjoy."

As it was, Margaret and I experienced a delightful evening with Prince Aly Khan: a soiree of fine wine, gourmet foods, and fascinating company. Sadly, his life would be cut short in an auto accident, on May 12, 1960, while driving a sports car much like the one he was in when we met. Aly Khan's passion for fast cars, racehorses, and beautiful women, deprived him of the honor to succeed his father, Aga Khan III, as the spiritual leader of 20 million Asian and African Ismaili Muslims.

Rita Hayworth & Prince Aly Khan, their Wedding Day (1949)

The dilemma of my being Jewish, and Margaret, a Catholic, was ongoing. She held fast to the dream of us being together for the rest of our lives. I knew deep down this could never be. At one point, she suggested we move to Australia or some other far-off country before our families caught on to us.

"And leave everything behind? Your posh lifestyle, my family's businesses, our parents and siblings? Since my brother returned from Israel last year, the Garbs are a family again. Mum and Dad would be heartbroken if I left Dublin now. Margaret, honestly, I have too much invested here to run off with you."

Her eyes showed disappointment, but she smiled, kissed me on the cheek, and said, "You're right, Theo," all the while conjuring ways for our relationship to succeed.

It was a small circle of friends who knew about us – Shloime, for one, and Michael, Margaret's brother, who I had the chance to meet on occasion with her, in a pub or on the streets of Dublin. He and his sister were close and shared each other's secrets. Michael, as I remember, was a jovial sort of fellow, and he and I became friendly. As Margaret came to know Shloime, she understood me better. She would ask him about Judaism and what it means to us as young Jewish men.

* * *

Now, there's an annual ball that takes place in Naas every spring honoring the Kildare Hunt. Begun by the Irish aristocracy in 1860, this festival is the social event of the year in Kildare County, even to this day. Margaret, adventurous as she was, suggested we all go together, including my brother Abe.

"Jews at a Hunt Ball?" Shloime said.

"It's not likely we'll run into anyone we know," I joked. Then turning to Margaret, "It *is* a little crazy. We've no business there."

"What do you mean no business? You're with me. That's all the business you need. Besides, Michael will be there. We'll have a smashing time!"

She paid the way for Shloime and me, buying our tickets and renting us red velvet jackets and fancy jodhpurs for the night.

"Ever think you'd dress up like this?" I asked Shloime, when we were decked out in our clothing.

He shook his head. "Not in my wildest dreams."

The ball took place in a huge, fairy-tale-like castle from a millennia ago. A sumptuous banquet was laid out on an enormous table, with brightly-lit crystal chandeliers casting a regal glow on the event. The Irish aristocracy was there, dressed to the nines, and so was an acquaintance of mine, Billy, a Dublin Jew, known to participate in equestrian events. Billy was an accomplished horseman who followed the hunt and played Polo among the Irish.

"What the f-ck are you doing here, Theo?" he asked, walking over to greet me.

I was startled to see him and quickly said, "Hey Billy, if it's good enough for you, it's good enough for me!" Although skeptical, he accepted my presence there.

My, did we have a ball! Dancing to Irish and popular music while feasting on a buffet of meats, fishes, salads and vegetables, and Irish potatoes, topped off with a Viennese table of mouth-watering desserts – I can tell you, the champagne and Guinness flowed that night! As delightful a time it was, I remember a heated argument with Margaret over religion, and how it threatened our future together; this was my belief. Margaret had a different view:

"You always make a bigger deal of it than it is," she said.

"No, I don't. It *is* a big deal."

She turned to Shloime. "Why must religion hold such power over our lives?"

Shloime looked at us both, stoically. "I don't think I should get involved."

What could I say? We were of different religions and social status, each with its exclusivities, and this would never change. Soon, our squabbles became familiar background noise to our relationship.

We continued our weekend getaways to country towns outside of Dublin. The innkeepers were good Catholics, God-fearing people of high moral character, who wanted no part of our sinful behavior. One vigilant fellow caught us in the midst of such conduct during our stay in Drogheda. He was just outside our rooms, perhaps with his ear to the door, when he heard us laughing. It happened that Margaret and I were frolicking in the bath.

"I'll have none of that here!" the man shouted from the hallway.

"Did you hear something?" I asked.

She listened, shook her head no, and continued laughing hysterically. Then came pounding on the door.

"Do you hear? None of that!!" I thought the latch would break any moment and the door fly open.

"Oh my God," Margaret said, covering herself with a bath towel.

"Bloody hell!" the man shouted. "You'll be out of here this minute! Out, I say!!"

The innkeeper went on and on in a good ol' Irish tantrum. Moving quickly, we gathered our things and fled. We entered the car, silent, somewhat chastened by the experience. I drove for a time without a word passing between us. After a few kilometers, Margaret giggled softly. "Did you see his face?"

I glanced at her and laughed. "I thought he might burst a gut!"

We were soon laughing ourselves silly over the incident, as we drove the narrow, winding roads back to Dublin.

Chapter 22

A Parting of Ways

Looking back on my relationship with Margaret, I am grateful for her sharing another world with me, a grand and elegant one. As well, she planted the seed of emigrating to Australia, and it was this idea that started to play in my mind, in early 1950. I loved Margaret with the fierce passion of a true first love and was going crazy over what to do about us.

A dear friend, Ronnie Sevitt, and his family, had moved to Sydney in 1948, and from the letters he wrote, they loved it there. Ronnie studied medicine in Dublin but never practiced it in Australia. Instead, he met a man, a Mr. Pettit, and they decided to build houses together for first-time homeowners. The Australian government was promoting immigration to their country; all would be welcome, Anglo-Saxons and Jews alike. Free passage and assistance in finding work or establishing a business were offered. At the age of twenty, I became excited with the prospect of moving to Sydney as well.

When I informed my parents of this, my father said, "If you think a better life is waiting for you there, we won't stop you." I was humbled to know they would support my decision to emigrate from Ireland. Leaving my family would be difficult enough for me, and I took solace in their understanding. After all, they had moved four times in search of a better life.

Lucy offered a different perspective: she suggested that if I was determined to go to Australia, I should first go to the United States and meet our cousins in New York, Chicago, and Los Angeles. Her point was, after I visit them, I can decide whether to continue on to Australia. I had to admit that America was an attractive option.

Since returning to Dublin, Abey became seriously involved with a Jewish girl by the name of Arlette Noyk. Her father was Michael Noyk, a famous Irish, Jewish solicitor. Now, true to his nature, Abe encouraged me to follow my heart when it came to Margaret. However, my heart was in turmoil, and his recent example of courting a Jewish girl made it even more difficult for me. How to escape the spell I was under! How to explain to her that I would be traveling alone, and to America first. My inner struggle led me to the decision that I must break clean of our relationship and leave Ireland; only then would I know my destiny. Wanderlust came naturally to me as it did my parents, and Abey, who had his adventures abroad. It was now my turn.

"What?!" Margaret shouted when I told her my plans.

"America and Australia. I'm thinking of going to them both – alone."

When she realized that I was serious, she said, "Theo, I love you. I want to share my life with you, have children with you. If this means converting to Judaism, then I am ready to do so for us."

"What do you mean?" I asked, knowing that even this large gesture on her part would not be enough.

"I'll start going to synagogue and begin learning about conversion with a Rabbi." Eventually, Margaret would attend synagogue weekly at a different shul than mine; there were three in Dublin. She reminded me of the fortune that she would inherit at twenty-one. "Once I've received my inheritance, we'll go to Australia together. We'll marry and then be off."

Margaret's proposal was gut-wrenching. I would possess the love of my life, untold wealth, and a bright future. On the other hand, our families, of different religions and social standing, would never accept one another. My parents would be denied *machatanim*, Jewish in-laws, who would celebrate with a full heart the wonderful life-cycle events and holidays, which mark time within a Jewish family – and I, too, the same. In my heart, I knew that family and tradition were paramount to a meaningful life for me.

* * *

July 10, 1950, my twenty-first birthday, is the day I chose for my departure to America. In the months leading up to that day, Margaret pleaded with me not to go. She was determined to keep me from leaving her and made such a fuss that I postponed my trip more than once. In fact, she convinced me to delay so many times that October came and went, and I hadn't a ticket in hand. Our tearful conversations are still painful to remember; I never doubted the sincerity of our love.

It was comical, returning to the Cunard Line office several times, either to purchase or cancel my ticket. They thought I was crazy. "There's the nut I was telling you about," one agent whispered to another. "Hello, young man. How can we help you today?"

Margaret thought she had won. That in the end, I would be hers. But though I wavered, I was determined to go. The ingrained message of my upbringing held sway. What would become of me if I didn't leave Ireland?

The thought of leaving Dublin, my family, and a hysterical Margaret behind, was so stressful to me that I began to wish we had never met. Distracted from work at the School of Motoring and my studies, I felt cut adrift from everything that was my anchor in life.

Friends argued against my leaving Ireland, and Shloime had plans for us to go into business together after college. "Theo, with your gift for gab and my vision for our success, we'll make a fortune together! Stay, and let's make a go of it." But despite the comfortable life I could have in Ireland, being close to family and venturing into business with Shloime, my decision was to leave.

Like a salmon that labors upstream to spawn her eggs, for me, tradition conquered love and called me to enter the fold of Judaism. More than religious observance, it was the subtle threads of family life during the weekly Sabbath, Jewish holidays, and special occasions, that I would miss.

We shared our last moments together in the town of Glendalough, from the Irish, *Gleann Da Loch* (valley of two lakes). Fitting indeed, as our lives would soon diverge. It was late November, the weekend before my departure, and saying goodbye was an agony; we were in tears much of the time. As we sat on a blanket by the lake, she turned her face to mine, misty-eyed, and said, "Please don't go."

I took her hands in mine. "Margaret, my darling, you are a glorious woman. One day you will meet a man who loves you, as I have loved you. Someone of your kind. A prince, who will give you the world."

She looked deeply into my eyes. "Meet a man? A prince who will give me the world? I already have." Margaret threw her arms around me. "Oh, Theo, can't we explore the world together?"

I held her tight, tighter and more closely than ever, knowing these were our last moments together. *If only you were Jewish, I would kneel on bended knee and ask for your hand.* But she was not. And I was what I was: a Jewish lad from Dublin.

We left Glendalough, Margaret in tears, and I, feeling awful for causing her sorrow. One last time, we drove up to the gates of her home. I let the engine idle...

"You'll write me?" she asked hopefully.

"No," I shook my head, "it must be a clean break, or we'll suffer for the rest of our lives."

I asked her not to come to the docks to see me off, as this would only upset her and draw the suspicion of my parents and others who'd wonder at the distress of a stranger (and an obviously Christian girl). We embraced, and then I watched as she disappeared behind the iron bars into a life separate from mine.

* * *

The day of my departure to America came – December 3, 1950 – an overcast yet mild winter's morning. At the harbor, a few dozen people gathered to see me off: family and friends, officials from the Jewish community, rabbis and teachers, and a few business associates who were there out of allegiance to my father. Some gave me the name of a loved one: a brother, a sister, a cousin, an aunt or uncle, who lived in America, who I "just have to" visit.

In the midst of so many goodbyes, I noticed a tall, slim figure emerge on the docks, walking at a brisk pace toward us. As she neared, *could it be?* ... *Margaret!* I caught my brother's eye and nodded a glance in her direction. *If she reaches me in tears and causes a scene!* Abe signaled that he would head off her intrusion. She may have intended a discreet goodbye, but I couldn't take that chance. Abey broke away from the crowd and intercepted her.

To this day, I don't know what words were exchanged, but he managed to turn her away without anyone knowing she was there. I looked once in her direction, and, in the same moment, she turned. Our eyes met. Smiling through her tears, she waved and then stepped off the dock and out of sight. . .

I hugged my family one last time, Ma and Sarah in tears, Lucy smiling, and Da, beaming with pride. Then Abey and I embraced, and with my lips to his ear, "Thank you, Abe. Close call."

He laughed. "Best of luck, Theo. Bon voyage and God bless."

Two suitcases in hand, I walked the gangplank onto the ship and waved goodbye to all who came to see me off. We sailed for England, where I stayed a week in the Cumberland Hotel at Hyde Park Corner, London, prior to boarding the Queen Mary at Southampton on December 9th – my destination, New York.

* * *

I was in London a few days, when there was a knock on my hotel room door. "Who is it?" I asked, thinking it was the maid.

"Theo, it's Shloime."

I was dumbfounded. What is Shloime doing here? Suddenly, I was gripped with fear, thinking it could only mean bad news from home. I opened the door, and there was Shloime looking grim.

"Hello, my friend," I said, wrapping my arms around him. I pulled back and looked him square in the eyes. "What brings you to London, Shloime?" I asked, expecting the worst possible news.

"Theo, it's Margaret. She swallowed a bottle of pills the day you left. But don't worry, she's out of danger now and resting comfortably in the hospital."

"My God, Shloime! Is she going to be all right?"

"Yes, yes, she will. A colleague at work found her in the employee bathroom, unconscious. They rushed her to the hospital and did what was necessary to save her."

I lay awake that night reliving my year and a half with Margaret: our electric first encounter, our secret trysts in town, romantic weekends in the country, dinner with Aly Khan, the Hunt Ball, and our last, tearful goodbye outside the gates of her home – these were sweet memories. I closed my eyes, affirmed a life decision to, one day, marry within my faith, and then, I prayed for her: *Mish'berach…*

As it was, Margaret made a full recovery. Sometime later, I heard that she had fallen from a horse and contracted pneumonia straight away; apparently the fall had weakened her lungs. Further on, tuberculosis set in, and she was hastened to a medical retreat in Switzerland, to be cured with gold injections.

Several years would pass before there was more news – good news for a change. She had married a solicitor in Dublin; the Irish Times ran the announcement. And this is the last I heard of her.

Epilogue

I arrived in New York December 14, 1950. At first, I stayed with my cousins, David and Dora Winderbaum, who lived in Brooklyn, at the intersection of Brooklyn and Church Avenues. Exhausted after the five-day crossing, it was good to be on dry land and coming home to family.

Their daughter, Celia, a college student, was at school when I arrived that day. The guest bedroom wasn't quite ready, so I lay down on her bed and immediately fell asleep. One of Celia's favorite stories is how she came home and found a stranger sleeping in her bed, ". . . and he's been there ever since!" A few years later, Celia and I were married.

My original plan was to travel across the U.S. to California and then make my way to Australia. But the long and short of it is, that, from my first glimpse of the Statue of Liberty, I fell in love with America. It may sound cliché, but no one should underestimate the power of seeing Lady Liberty after a five-day ocean voyage. Other considerations persuaded me to stay in Brooklyn: my growing fondness for Celia and my relatives owning a furniture store, Reliable Upholsterers – and so, the potential for a wife and a career.

From the moment I stepped off the boat, I was charmed, despite the heartache of recent events. In those first months, I was drenched with thoughts of Margaret's well-being, but resisted contacting her. The last thing I wanted was to cause her further pain. I was in America about a year, when Shloime wrote to me with the news of Margaret's fall and subsequent illnesses; I felt terrible for her. When my cousins asked if everything was all right, I said, "Just some news about an old friend."

Celia Winderbaum, Coney Island, NY (1949)

What else could I say? As the weeks and months passed, my life centered more in the present and the future, and less in the past. Two years later, all of that shifted again. On March 11, 1953, I received a Western Union cable from home: "Father died of heart attack 4 a.m. Tuesday. Funeral 4:45 p.m. Garb family." Da was but fifty-three years young.

Without warning, the dominant presence in my life was gone. Although I flew back to Dublin as soon as possible, I arrived after the funeral; in keeping with Jewish law, my father was buried the same day he died. Over the next several months, I joined my family in mourning our great loss, and assisted my siblings in putting Da's affairs in order, making sure that our mother would always be cared for.

* * *

Some years later while on a visit to see Ma, I drove to the town where Margaret's family had lived. It was a small community, one that noticed strangers and regarded them with suspicion. I sat in a pub for well over an hour, sipping a Guinness, enduring the stares of the bartender and the locals, each silently asking: *what is he doing here*? Finally, I summoned enough courage to ask the bartender if he knew of Margaret or her family.

"Who wants to know?" the bartender asked with disdain. A number of patrons shifted in their seats, holding me in their gaze.

"I don't mean any harm. I'd been friendly with her and her brother, that's all." My voice trailed off, "Well, never mind."

I finished my beer and left the pub, glancing over my shoulder more than once as I found my car and drove off. This chapter in my life, full of passion and secrecy, would open and close, and become a faint memory – so faint, that thinking back, I wonder: *did it ever happen at all?*

But isn't that the way it is with the past? Even now, the sound of my father's dramatic tenor will rise up in memory, only to vanish like a wisp of smoke in the breeze. Sitting with the milkman as he delivered to homes by horse and buggy; running on the beach at Wicklow; the gatherings in our home during the war; my adventure in Paris; my early loves; Abey's rebellion and heroism; Margaret – all fading memories. Photographs and letters remind me of them, but the vault that stores these wonderful memories, in all their many colors, is my heart.

* * *

My mother, Rachel Garb, lived in Dublin as a widow until her passing in 1984, at the age of eighty-five. Although she had various offers to remarry, she was faithful to Wolf's memory. My son, Michael, recalls that his "Nanny Ray" once shared with him, "Do you know why I was faithful to your grandfather all those years after he died? He would say to me, 'Rachel, you are my rose.'" Ma is buried in the Dublin Jewish cemetery along with Da, and Zeyde as well.

What of my brother and sisters? Shloime and myself? We all traveled different paths: Abe married Welsh stage actress, playwright, and director, Evelyn Bowen, fathered two boys, David and Richard, and emigrated to Halifax, Nova Scotia, in 1956. Later on, he divorced and moved to Toronto, Canada, where he now lives with his wife,

Mary, and her daughter, Teri. Abe returned to school for his engineering degree and had a career of note as a civil engineer and college professor.

Lucy married Henry, a Jewish Scotsman from Glasgow, a "Jack of all trades," followed Abe to Toronto and raised two boys there, William and Howard. Lucy taught piano her whole life, preparing students for recitals and competitions. She passed away in 2003, several years after Henry.

Sarah and Bevan left Ireland to live in Paris, France, where they raised four children (Bernard, William, Vivianne, and Jennifer). Bevan became a diplomat and star economist for the OECD in France, while Sarah taught English to bankers and played hostess to foreign dignitaries. They resided half the year in Paris and half the year in Nice, France, until 2010, when Bevan passed away in his sleep. Since then, Sarah has lived alone in Paris until this day, painting, a great passion of hers. Her daughter, Jennifer, looks after her.

Shloime never left Ireland. Instead, he married and went into business there and earned the fortune he spoke of, manufacturing women's pocketbooks and fashion accessories. We get together now and then, either here in New York, or in Dublin, and speak on the telephone, wishing each other a "good yom tov" on Jewish holidays.

Theo, Celia, and Shloime, New York (1960s)

As for myself, well, Celia and I have five children: William born in 1956, Michael and Sharon, some years later, and (Michael's and Sharon's) spouses, Isabella and Robert. Our grandchildren are Aaron and Evan. My career followed this path: I learned the furniture business and became a decorator, providing customers with home furnishings and interior design. In 1968, I entered the stock market as a broker, servicing clients until the market crash of 1973. It was then that I decided to fulfill my lifelong dream of living in Israel.

Although my wife was uncertain (her life in New York, rich with friends and a career), our children were game for an adventure. I persuaded Celia to take a sabbatical from teaching and experience life in Israel for one year, exploring the possibility of our family making *aliyah* (settling there).

In the summer of 1973, the Garbs left Bayberry Lane in Seaford for a true adventure in the Holy Land. Within six weeks of our arrival, on Yom Kippur, as the whole country prayed in synagogue, the Arab nations attacked Israel, in what would become known as the Yom Kippur War. We found ourselves running to bomb shelters for safety and volunteering in the war effort.

I owned a car there and transported food and medical supplies to the soldiers at the front. Michael, who was a Bar Mitzvah that year, recalls loading our Citroen hatchback to the ceiling with cases of Hershey's chocolate bars and, on another occasion, bandages and medicines, delivering them from warehouses to the army camps at the front lines of battle.

We returned home in August 1974, and, although Celia and I visit frequently, we never did make aliyah. Subsequently, I returned to the furniture industry until my retirement in 1991 and have enjoyed spending quality time with my grandchildren, sailing, playing tennis, acting in Gilbert and Sullivan's Yiddish Light Opera Company, and giving talks – at libraries, special interest clubs, and synagogues – about my life, growing up Jewish in Ireland.

In 1995, my son Michael's good friend and business partner then, Eric, gave Michael a 35th birthday present of a father-and-son trip to Ireland. It was a bonding experience and a fabulous time, sharing with him my childhood home (now a bed-and-breakfast) and the apple trees my father planted there, the remnants of Greenville Hall, our summer home in Wicklow, the beautiful Irish countryside, as well as introducing him to friends of my youth.

We surviving Garbs now live in different parts of the world. Are you surprised? We are descended from wanderers. Rarely do we manage to return to Ireland, our beloved emerald ark.

Even so, we honor our twin heritage of faith and love of country, and the memory of those who have bestowed upon us a rich inheritance.

Irish Jews? Yes, indeed! Irish Jews.

LUCY – THEO – SARAH – ABE – LONDON 1993

Editor's Note

Emerald Ark, Memories of a Jewish Irish Youth, a memoir, is being published posthumously. My father, Theo Garb, passed away on December 18, 2014, at the age of 85, after an eight-year battle with progressive dementia. His book has lain dormant for eighteen years and comes to light only now, as I have recently become inspired to revisit and edit the original draft of dad's manuscript, ensuring that Theo's "voice" tells his story. It has been a labor of love.

A few people have contributed to the writing of this book and deserve mention. They are author Greg Lawrence, who worked closely with Theo in developing a first draft of the manuscript; my English professor, Christopher Hobson (SUNY College at Old Westbury), who guided me with astute comments on capturing the emotional beats of a narrative; and Theo's lifelong friend, Eli Shaff, who lent his hand to copy editing parts of the original draft.

I trust you have enjoyed reading dad's story. His brother, Abe, now 99 years young, is currently writing *his* memoirs, which hopefully, one day, will be in your hands as well :)

Peace & Blessings,

Michael M. Garb, Editor

www.michaelmgarb.com
cantormike18@gmail.com

P.S. If you wish to own mp3 music files of Theo and Abe singing Irish, Yiddish, and Hebrew songs ("home" recordings) and rare historic recordings of Cantor Rev. Wolf Garb's chanting, please go to: www.michaelmgarb.com and follow link to "audiobook."

Addt'l Photographs

Celia & Theo, Dublin, Ireland (1952)

The Wedding of Sarah Garb & Bevan Stein, Dublin (1952)
(Celia Winderbaum, to right of Wolf; Theo, behind and to left of groom; Lucy to right of Abe)

Celia Garb, 92 Years Young (2022)

'OY VEY 'Z MIR'

Photo by Kevin Graff

Theo Garb delighted his audience with the Yiddish version of songs from Gilbert and Sullivan operettas Wednesday in the Truesdale Room at Hurlbut Church. Garb is a member of the Yiddish Gilbert and Sullivan Light Opera Company of Long Island. He entertained the Chautauqua Hebrew congregation and their friends.

Theo Garb "Growing Up Jewish in Ireland" Lecture
Chautauqua, NY (2000)

Theo Garb in the Yiddish Version of Gilbert & Sullivan's
"H.M.S. Pinafore" (1990s)

Concert Poster reads: "Wolf Garbarz, the Esteemed Cantor from Manchester, England, in Concert, July 27–28, 1930, Warsaw, Poland, in Dedication of the New Hospital"

Uncle Leon "Leibele" Garbarz (1902-1942)
Warsaw, circa late 1930s
Died with Wife & Children in Treblinka Death Camp
After the "liquidation" of the Warsaw Ghetto

Uncle Aron Garbarz (1915-1943)

Warsaw (1936)

Died with Wife & Children in Majdanek Death Camp

Lublin, Poland

Taube Welt Rosenstrauch (w/umbrella and 3 of her 4 children) left to right: Rachel, Miriam, and Harry (unknown cousin to left) The only survivor of the Holocaust: Rachel Rosenstrauch Garb

"Shattered"

Krajdsztejn (Kreitstein) Family (Celia's Grandparents)

*Top Row: Tante Sura & Dora (Celia's mother, on right)
Seated: Szuel & Chana Liba Krajdsztejn*

Boy: Mattis Moshe Krajdsztejn (for whom Michael is named)

Dora was one of nine siblings. All perished in the Holocaust except for Dora, Sura, and Roiska (not pictured). These three came to America and lived long, healthy lives, having children and grandchildren...

Uncle Rev. David Garb (1910-1967) with Children

Louis & Shana (Jean, top right)

Bar Mitzvah of Louis Garb, Blackpool, England (1947)

Aunt Jean & Husband, Shalom Freedland

London (September 1949)

Cantor Rev. Wolf Garb, Danziger & Kalmanowitz Wedding
New York, NY (1947)

Eire Sanctuary for Jews, Sends Food, Says Dublin Cantor on Visit to Hub

BOSTON TRAVELER By ALTA MALONEY

Ireland, "the only country in Europe where Jewish blood has not been spilled through the centuries," now is extending sympathetic help to the displaced persons on the continent.

EIRE GAVE MEAT

The Rev. Wolf Garb, chief cantor of the United Hebrew Congregation in Dublin, explains some of the understanding that his Catholic and Protestant neighbors have for the Jewish situation by drawing a parallel between the Irish nation's and Jewish people's fight for survival.

The cantor, who was invited here to conduct services at the Temple Mishkan Tefila, Roxbury, says that even the government of Eire is awake to the problem. Recently it allocated 1,000,000 pounds of kosher meat for Jewish displaced persons in Germany.

In addition, the government has made it easy for the Jewish people in Dublin to bring relatives into the country. Members of the cantor's community, of 1000 families in Dublin have received permits for relatives in concentration camps to enter the country within a few days of application.

A naturalized Irish citizen, Cantor Garb says there is "no Jewish problem" in Eire. His people there are very happy, he declares, and have no wish to move, even to come to the United States.

But the war is still going on over there, the cantor declares—"There is no peace yet." In the tea and clothing allotments in their own country, however, the members of the Jewish community and their friends of other faiths are sending food parcels to the Continent.

During the war, some 70 refugees who farmed about 400 acres of Northern Ireland contributed, according to Dublin's chief cantor, "millions of ... tatoes and millions of ... vegtables to the war effort.

"They were not only self-supporting, but they produced for the country."

200 DIE IN FAMILY

Cantor Garb has real knowledge of his people's problems in many countries of Europe. His own family is almost a United Nations in itself. Born in Warsaw, Poland, he came to Dublin by way of Antwerp, Belgium, and Manchester, England. His four children, one born in each of the countries, are of different nationalities.

In his own family, the cantor counts 200 members dead in war atrocities—most in the city of Warsaw. A brother, who survived is a rabbi now in Manchester, England.

"You people don't realize what it means to come to America," he says. He and his wife have many friends.

THE REV. WOLF GARB

country and will visit them before returning to Ireland.

"But once you visit America, Cantor Garb says,"—it has a magnetism that draws you to visit

---

"But once you visit America," Cantor Garb says,

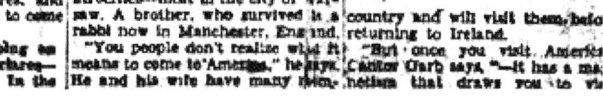

"it has a magnetism that draws you to visit again."

The Boston Evening Traveller (1947)

THE REV. WOLF GARB

Mr. PHILIP MODDEL writes: Dublin Jewry has been shocked by the sudden death of the Rev. Wolf Garb, at the age of 52. At his funeral, which was attended by a large gathering, Rabbi I. Jakobovits, Chief Rabbi of Eire, paid a tribute to him. Mr. Garb, before entering business in 1947, was First Reader of the United Hebrew Congregation for a period of 18 years, he had previously served congregations in Manchester and London. A native of Warsaw, Mr. Garb employed his magnificent voice for the traditional rendering of the services in a most pleasing way. He was always ready to respond to requests to grace social and other gatherings with his attractive Hebrew and Yiddish melodies, and he took a very active interest in the Dublin Jewish Musical Society, the choir of which he joined at the Israeli Zimriyah last year."

Rev. Wolf Garb Obituary

Jewish Press, Ireland (March 1953)

Wolf on the Streets of Frankfurt, Germany (1951)

Exploring the Ring of Kerry

County Kerry, Ireland

Father-and-Son Trip to Ireland (1995)

Standing Among Apple Trees My Grandfather Planted in 1930
97 Donore Terrace (opposite Greenville Hall Synagogue)

"Shmoozing with Irish Youth over a Guinness"

Davy Byrnes Pub, Dublin City

(Author James Joyce's "old haunt")

Printed in Great Britain
by Amazon